WHAT PEOPLE ARE SAYING ABOUT

ALONG *the* WAY

"We are all on a journey. Randy Hain's book is an insightful and engaging look at his journey as a Catholic that is filled with helpful observations and lessons. *Along the Way* is an excellent road map for lifelong Catholics, converts, reverts, or anyone simply seeking the Truth that can only be found in the Church. This is a book I recommend reading more than once and giving a copy to everyone you know."

—**Matthew Kelly,** *The New York Times* best-selling author of *Rediscover Catholicism*

"Life is a journey, especially for Christians. We are sojourners on a pilgrimage toward heaven. As Randy Hain illustrates so beautifully in *Along the Way*, it is up to us to make this one-time trip a truly authentic one. If we want to make the most of these earthly travels we need to put Jesus and his Church in the driver's seat. This book is a must-have manual to help us do just that."

—**Teresa Tomeo,** syndicated Catholic talk show host and best-selling Catholic author

"Whether you are a lifelong Catholic or a seeker trying to make sense of life's greatest mysteries, let Randy Hain's phenomenal book *Along the Way: Lessons for an Authentic Journey of Faith* be the road map for your spiritual adventures. Hain, a convert with a commitment to living a fully integrated and authentic life, addresses many of the faith's most challenging issues head on with honesty. Randy shares his own obstacles and tribulations, but he also delivers tremendous tools and suggestions for making the most of this life we're given. As someone who is 'along the way' to my desired eternal destination, I'm thrilled to have a spiritual guide like Randy Hain to help me make the most of this journey."

—**Lisa M. Hendey,** founder of CatholicMom.com and author of *A Book of Saints for Catholic Moms*

"Besides liturgical renewal, the greatest lasting effect of the Second Vatican Council on the part of the laity is perhaps the rediscovery of the Universal Call to Holiness. It is a recognition that the greatest destiny that we have as Catholics is not to an earthly power and prestige, but to our ultimate home, in heaven.

"Despite this rediscovery, in the years since the council, there continues to be a great lack in the awareness of this call on the part of many laity, and many of the works of 'popular theology' seem to miss the target in addressing this call. Either they veer off into 'theological mumbo jumbo' that does not address the real-life situation of twenty-first-century Catholics, or they fall into the even deadlier trap of mixing in questionable practices and sources that, at best, cannot be called Christian.

"Into this void, Randy Hain's latest, *Along the Way*, weaves an appropriate amount of biographical details with solid, faithful catechetical teaching that reaches across the plain of socioeconomic divide to help all Catholic Christians who are struggling to live their lives in the public square in an authentic and true manner. Punctuated by excellent 'action items' that give concrete steps to putting our faith in action, Mr. Hain helps us all to recognize how Jesus truly does walk with us along the path of our pilgrimage of life while simultaneously helping us to also make him known to our brothers and sisters in Christ, that we might truly become a leaven for our society."
—**Father Kyle Schnippel**, director of vocations,
Archdiocese of Cincinnati

"*Along the Way* is a wonderfully comprehensive approach for growing in your relationship with Christ. Like Michelangelo seeing the final image in a piece of marble, so God sees you as complete in him. Randy's sound advice and insight will help you along the way."
—**Jeff Cavins**, creator of the *Great Adventure Bible Study Series*, author of *My Life on the Rock*, *Walking With God* and co-editor of the *Amazing Grace*™ series of books. He is the director of the Archbishop Harry J. Flynn Catechetical Institute in St. Paul, Minnesota.

"Randy Hain delivers a deeply personal, powerful account of his conversion to Catholicism—and his reasons for his devotion to the Church. *Along the Way* is a convincing read. Hain wants his readers to experience a true 'conversion of soul.' He moves from his entry into the Church to his evolution as a new Catholic. He candidly shares his struggles and provides the reader with timeless lessons throughout the book. The Atlanta-based businessman also relates how his newfound Catholic faith has affected his work and family. He shares lessons learned as an executive—especially keeping his priorities in check: God first, family second, and work next. Hain writes for men, women, parents, business people, and anyone who wants to deepen his or her spiritual life. Above all, he calls his readers to live their Catholic faith with courage, to embrace an 'integrated' Catholic life, and to rejoice in all that the Lord has for them."

—**Patrick Novecosky,**
editor-in-chief, *Legatus Magazine*

"*Along the Way: Lessons for an Authentic Journey of Faith* provides practical thoughts and ideas on how to integrate our spiritual lives into our day-to-day activities. Randy takes us on his journey and shares with us as he learns to use simple techniques that seamlessly blend faith, family and work. For those who think they don't have the time or the tools to put Christ into all aspects of their lives, this book is for you!"

—**Father Francis G. McNamee**, pastor,
Cathedral of Christ the King, Atlanta

"In this book we read the sincere words of a pilgrim for our time who knows all too well the temptations of money, power, and success. His spiritual journey to a renewed faith reveals the transformative and healing powers of the Catholic Church. At turns warm and insistent, humble and provocative, this book is a good compass for all of our restless hearts that need a map back to our source and end."

—**Phillip M. Thompson,** JD,PhD,LLM,
executive director of the Aquinas Center
of Theology at Emory University

"Randy's work in *Along the Way* will no doubt yield great benefit to many who are looking for insight and perspective into their journey of faith. Randy's style is clear, direct, interesting, and most importantly, practical. If you wrestle with the challenges of learning how to live out your Catholic faith in the midst of the overwhelming busy-ness of modern life, this book will no doubt provide you with the necessary perspective and encouragement to take your next step of faith."

—**Dan Burke**, executive director, National Catholic Register; author of *Navigating the Interior Life—Spiritual Direction and the Journey to God*

"Lay people can evangelize in ways we priests find impossible. So it is with Randy Hain. A former Southern Baptist, Randy combines a passion for Christ and his Church with the practical mind of a successful businessman and the ability to communicate with clarity and from the heart. *Along the Way* is an indispensable guidebook to walk in the way of Christ the Lord, who is himself the way to eternal life. Highly recommended!"

—**Father Dwight Longenecker**, author of *The Quest for the Creed*, blogger, broadcaster, and pastor of Our Lady of the Rosary parish in Greenville, South Carolina

"Just as Pope Benedict XVI proclaims a year of faith, Randy Hain writes of his Catholic faith with the white-hot intensity of the newly converted. *Along the Way* is reminiscent of Saint Paul's power and passion. Paul meant it when he wrote, "To me, life is Christ" (Philippians 1:21). These words take form and shape between the covers of *Along the Way*. The integrity of the testimony, the authenticity of the message, the urgent need for this message now all join together in making Randy Hain's new book a must-read. Following after his award-winning *The Catholic Briefcase* (2011), the book complements and continues its theme of living the integrated Catholic life. 'If but ten among us lead a holy life, we shall kindle a fire which will light up the entire city (Saint John Chrysostom).'"

—**Sister Timothy Marie, OCD,** co-editor of *Spirit of Carmel Magazine*, Carmelite Sisters of the Most Sacred Heart of Los Angeles

"As Christians, we are all disciples on our own way to Emmaus in search of Jesus Christ. In his book *Along the Way*, lay Catholic writer Randy Hain provides valuable insight to help assist us as we each continue this journey, wherever we may be on that road. Like a good teacher, Randy brings our rich Catholic faith and practical applications of the Sermon on the Mount alive for us. He shows examples through prayer, Scripture, and devotions of easy ways in allowing God and the Holy Spirit to become a part of our work and family life each day. Regardless if you are a cultural, habitual, or committed Catholic, Randy's suggestions, recommendations, and lessons learned in *Along the Way* will help strengthen your resolve to finish the journey."

> —**Joseph J. Krygiel**, chief executive officer of Catholic Charities Atlanta

"Much more than one man's journey—in *Along the Way*, author Randy Hain openly shares his 'ordinary' life of struggles and searching which ultimately results in his surrender to Christ and a fulfilling Catholic life. Hain presents a crisp road map to illuminate a pilgrim's path, leading the way to authentic Truth found in the Catholic Church."

> —**Donna-Marie Cooper O'Boyle**, EWTN TV host and author of numerous Catholic books, including *Rooted in Love: Our Calling as Catholic Women*

"*Along the Way* is the handbook for everyone who is journeying—and struggling—along the path of conversion. Randy Hain guides each of us and reminds us of the importance of not giving up or considering ourselves done with conversion. He also brings a healthy dose of real life and practical advice (and maybe a bit of humor). Not only will you enjoy reading this book, you'll find yourself a better person for it!"

> —**Sarah Reinhard**, author of *A Catholic Mother's Companion to Pregnancy: Walking with Mary from Conception to Baptism*, and online at SnoringScholar.com

"Randy Hain's conversion to the Catholic faith after twenty-three years of drifting without any faith practice is a testimony to God's infinite love for finite man. How God pursues us and waits for decades even when we deny his very existence, living a hedonistic lifestyle, he still waits! From Southern Baptist to agnostic, hedonist, and workaholic, Randy Hain captures the true meaning of life and peace that can only be found in a deep relationship with the one who created us! Randy has found the source and summit of everyday existence where few dare to pursue.

"*Along the Way* is a road map clearly and concisely written not just for converts and Catholics but for any Christian seeking a closer walk with the Lord. No matter how busy a schedule we keep, Randy shows how to prioritize and organize our days to make time to be with the Lord, the most important aspect of our lives. It's good for the soul, from cover to cover."

—**Edward J. Daccarett**, publisher, Christian Action
News; and general manager, Prince of Peace Catholic
Radio

"*Along the Way* provides readers with a real and practical road map to the Catholic Church, revealing its beauty, value, and relevancy for a meaningful and purpose-filled life. This is a must-read for anyone exploring the Church or for those who are seeking more than what modern culture offers for personal fulfillment."

—**Kate Sell**, Catholic strategist and development
professional; owner, KLS Strategies, LLC

"*Along the Way* delivers on its title. This highly accessible book will not only show you that your challenges, reservations, and struggles along your faith journey are not unique, the book will also provide you with the tools, guidance, and inspiration to keep going on your way. Reading Randy Hain's faith journey is at once familiar and humbling. His challenges along the way are the former, the degree of his commitment to apply his new found faith the latter. Truly inspiring!"

—**Andreas Widmer**, author of *The Pope and the CEO*
and co-founder of the SEVEN Fund

"Randy Hain is a man on a mission. He's a good friend and kindred spirit when it comes to integrating faith and work, but there's something truly remarkable about his writing. Randy has an astonishing gift of blending real-world experience, solid Catholic teaching, and a deep humility. The result is this book, where he discusses the journey of life and faith in a way that will leave a mark on our souls. *Along the Way: Lessons for an Authentic Journey of Faith* is a treasure, filled with practical and spiritual insights. Read, love it, and live it."

—**Kevin Lowry**, chief operating officer, The Coming Home Network International, and author, *Faith at Work: Finding Purpose Beyond the Paycheck*

"Randy's ability to immediately disarm people and relate to their circumstances comes through in the first paragraph of this book. Converts, reverts, and lifelong committed Catholics will no doubt see themselves in the pages of Randy's work, as his experiences and personal development mirror what so many of us wrestle with in our search to find out why we're here. He and I have walked what might to outsiders seem like very different paths, but as I read *Along the Way*, I felt like I was re-reading my own journey toward the truth."

—**Matt Swaim**, producer, *The Son Rise Morning Show* on EWTN Radio, and author of *The Eucharist and the Rosary* and *Prayer in the Digital Age*

"Even a pagan like Socrates knew that 'the unexamined life is not worth living.' Augustine showed us how to make such an examination in God's presence. And Randy Hain shows us how to do it in the modern world, as a spouse and parent."

—**Mike Aquilina**, EWTN host and author of more than thirty Catholics books

ALONG *the* WAY | Lessons for an Authentic Journey of Faith

Randy Hain

Foreword by Tom Peterson

Liguori

LIGUORI, MISSOURI

Imprimi Potest:
Harry Grile, CSsR, Provincial
Denver Province, The Redemptorists

Published by Liguori Publications
Liguori, Missouri 63057

To order, call 800-325-9521
www.liguori.org

Library of Congress Cataloging-in-Publication Data

Hain, Randy.
 Along the way : lessons for an authentic journey of faith / Randy Hain ; foreword by Tom Peterson.—1st ed.
 p. cm.
 1. Christian life—Catholic authors. I. Title.
 BX2350.3.H35 2012
 248.4'82—dc23
                                                                          2012030262
 p ISBN 978-0-7648-2164-6
 e ISBN 978-0-7648-6742-2

Liguori Publications, a nonprofit corporation, is an apostolate of The Redemptorists. To learn more about The Redemptorists, visit Redemptorists.com.

Printed in the United States of America
16 15 14 13 12 / 5 4 3 2 1
First Edition

*This book is dedicated to my wife, Sandra,
and our sons, Alex and Ryan.
I am so grateful we are making this journey together.*

I love you very much.

Contents

Acknowledgments

No book is ever written alone. I am most grateful to our Lord for the second chance he gave me in 2005 and for inspiring me to share my experiences with others. I am incredibly grateful to my wonderful wife and sons for their love and support; they are my bedrock. My sincere thanks also go to Deacon Mike Bickerstaff for his mentoring, friendship, and collaboration since my conversion into the Church. He has had a tremendous influence on my life and the growth of my faith.

Cathy Bickerstaff was instrumental in helping me shape the early draft of the manuscript a few years ago, and her sound advice and editing help was the catalyst that launched this project. My friend, Lisa Guthrie of Grammar She Wrote, worked with me on *The Catholic Briefcase: Tools for Integrating Faith and Work,* and her expert editing and counsel was invaluable in developing *Along the Way.*

Catherine Fuss, Joe Krygiel, Kate Sell, Sarah Reinhard, Brian Campbell, Theresa Thomas, Sarah Vabulas, Matt Tovrog—thank you for your encouragement and helpful feedback in writing this book.

My sincere thanks go to Chris Findley for his collaboration on a very early version of chapter four (*A Journey Toward the Truth*). His faith journey has long been an inspiration to me. Tom Peterson, thank you for your friendship and the tremendous impact you are having in the Catholic world through Catholics Come Home and Virtue Media. Others who have inspired me through their writings or personal example include Dr. Peter Kreeft, Father Robert Barron, Patrick Lencioni, Kevin Lowry, Lisa Hendey, Dr. Paul Voss, Dan Spencer, Dr. Bill Thierfelder, Matt Swaim, Alex Muñoz, David Mc-

Cullough, Dr. Ron Young, Terry Trout, Brian Dooling, Price Harding, Paige Barry, Teresa Tomeo, and my father, Steve Hain.

I am blessed to know some wonderful priests who have made a positive difference in my life and am grateful for the significant influence they have had on my faith journey. Thank you, Father Henry Atem, Father Jim Flanagan, Father Dan Ketter and Father Peter Rau! The priest who will always be remembered by me and my family with much love and appreciation is Father Frank McNamee, who welcomed us into the Church, baptized our children and convalidated our marriage. From the first time my wife and I met him in the summer of 2005, Father Frank served as our guiding shepherd, and we will be forever grateful for his generosity, wisdom, and positive influence in our lives.

I am most grateful to our Lord Jesus Christ and pray that everything about this book and my faith journey in the Catholic Church reflects honor and glory back to him.

Foreword

Whether you are traveling to a new international destination, hiking through a densely wooded forest, or exploring any unfamiliar terrain, it's always more enjoyable when you have a traveling companion who knows the way. That person has the advantage of having been there before, showing you the shortcuts and the best route, helping to reduce the stress and uncertainty of the unknown.

The same is true with our spiritual journey of faith. We can all benefit from straightforward and essential coaching, which helps what might have been a long and sometimes complicated odyssey to become a much more exciting and enjoyable adventure! In *Along the Way: Lessons for an Authentic Journey of Faith*, Randy Hain is your spiritual companion, and he has written a wonderful guide filled with practical and helpful insights as you continue your walk closer to Christ.

As a friend and a fellow parishioner since 2006, I've witnessed Randy's heart for our Lord and his conversion to the Catholic faith. Randy is a "marathon man," not literally as a runner but as a disciple of Jesus, filled with fortitude and passion. His gaze is firmly affixed on the finish line of heaven, and he wants nothing more than to assist all of us along the way to get there as well.

As the author and our guide, Randy is unwavering in his pursuit for spiritual knowledge, a quest for excellence, and a passionate desire to bring the Good News of Jesus to a world in need of hope. Randy's heart is singularly focused, and he has his priorities in the right order. He is consistent in his service and dedication to those people God puts in his path. Having overcome personal doubts of faith, family health struggles, and career challenges himself, Randy can offer some wise counsel to help you navigate around the roadblocks and pitfalls along the way.

Having spent my thirty-five-year career in advertising, and more recently as founder and president of Catholics Come Home®, I can honestly say that Randy truly strives to live an authentic Christian life each day. As a relatively new Catholic, his dedication to the Church is already noteworthy, serving as co-founder of the Annual Atlanta Catholic Business Conference and co-founder of the popular *Integrated Catholic Life* eMagazine. He is also the author of *The Catholic Briefcase: Tools for Integrating Faith and Work* (Liguori: 2011), which was named the Best Catholic Book of 2011 in the About.com Reader's Choice Awards.

Randy would be the first to tell you his unequaled drive for the new evangelization comes exclusively from the sacramental graces of our Lord working in his life and family.

In the chapters ahead, you will find easy-to-understand, concise examples for growing in your faith. You will discover answers to the everyday dilemmas we all face in life and help with common struggles that most of us encounter in our secular culture. As you progress along the way, you will uncover simple methods of reducing anxiety, increasing your prayer time, adding more joy in your daily life, and growing closer in your relationship with the living Christ.

By the end of your exploration through the pages that follow, you will discover that Randy wants nothing more than to encourage you to join him on the road less traveled while getting the most out of your own journey of faith.

Tom Peterson,
Founder and president of Catholics Come Home

Introduction

If you had told me ten years ago I would one day write a book about the lessons I learned on my faith journey, I would have laughed and walked away. At that time I had no faith in my life and rarely thought of having a relationship with God. But a series of events driven by a search for Truth was the catalyst for a profound personal conversion in 2005 that led my family and me into the Catholic Church.

Along the Way is about my faith journey and the lessons I have learned. All meaningful journeys have destinations. Where will mine take me? I know we are called to lead lives of holiness, and we are made for heaven, not the world. Despite feeling unworthy most days, I realize that I must be faithful, humble, obedient, loving, and actively engaged in the practice of my Catholic faith for me to reach my goal. I am also called to share the Good News with others.

Most productive journeys have road maps to guide travelers on their way. I feel incredibly blessed to have found the Catholic Church after living more than two decades with no faith in my life. Almost at the same time as my reception into the Catholic Church in 2006, I began writing about my faith experiences. This book is a candid and practical retelling of the lessons I have learned on my journey, my struggles, the knowledge I have gained, and how I have applied the teachings of the Catholic Church in my daily life. I hope the sharing of these experiences will illuminate the path and provide that road map for other Catholics and seekers of the Truth, a Truth that can only be found in our beautiful Catholic Church.

The book is not written chronologically but is instead broken into the four main parts of my faith journey. Part One candidly shares my conversion story and my journey to find the Truth. Part Two addresses the big issues I faced coming into the Church as I was introduced to reconciliation, evangelization, the Blessed Mother and the saints...among other things. The places where I have struggled on my journey are addressed in Part Three, and Part Four shares the path I am trying to follow toward an authentic, courageous, and integrated Catholic life.

As the title of this book implies, I view myself as a pilgrim on a continuing journey to seek and live in the Truth. In the early days of my conversion I intended to wrap my mind around the vast body of knowledge within the Church, but I quickly realized I would never learn everything there is to know about Catholicism. Instead, I chose to trust in the authority and teaching of the Church and the magisterium, knowing that my full understanding may take a lifetime. Even though I often stumble, this trust has enabled me to focus more fully on my faith journey and the experiences that have transformed my life. My intent in this book is to honestly and transparently share how making Christ the center of my life and fully embracing his Church have profoundly changed me for the better, and encourage others to more fully appreciate and live out their faith in authentic and courageous ways.

I pray that the Holy Spirit will work through what I have written to influence the men and women who read this book to experience a deeper relationship with Christ and the truth and beauty of his Church.

Part One

SURRENDER, PRIORITIES, *and* TRUTH

CHAPTER 1

Conversion

Out of the Spiritual Wilderness

"Jesus, I don't know what to do anymore and I need your help. I surrender. Please lead…and I will follow."

I FEEL INCREDIBLY BLESSED to have found the Truth of the Catholic Church at the age of forty after spending more than two decades in what I call the "spiritual wilderness," a time when I had no faith in my life. My departure from God began in my teen years as I started to have serious doubts about my compatibility with the Baptist Church, which I stopped attending at the age of sixteen. This rebellion then evolved to my declaring in college that I was an agnostic and later spending years as a workaholic who was too busy for God. A familiar tale, perhaps?

After moving from Annapolis, Maryland, to a small town in south Georgia when I was eight years old, my parents became very involved in a local Baptist church. My earliest memory of this time was being baptized when I was nine and going to the altar to be "saved." I enjoyed Sunday school and knew the Bible better than most adults.

As a teenager, I still attended church but was starting to feel that I didn't belong. I thought our preacher was making everything up as he went along during his sermons, and God's message was getting lost in his inclination to put on a show every Sunday. When I was sixteen, I announced to my parents that I didn't want to go to church anymore. We argued about it, but they had taught me to think for myself. They permitted me to stop attending, even though my decision clearly hurt them. Their own faith and involvement in church was stronger than ever, and I think they believed I would return soon. I remember thinking that my withdrawal from church life would be short-lived as well. Little did any of us know that I was about to leave my relationship with God for a *very* long time.

> *"The* LORD *is with me to the end.* LORD, *your mercy endures forever. Never forsake the work of your hands!"*
>
> PSALM 138:8

I graduated high school and went off to the University of Georgia on a partial scholarship, grant money, money my parents had scraped together, and student loans. I also worked a number of jobs in school to help pay expenses. My grades suffered as I thought of nothing other than having a good time with my friends. I would describe my college years as the darkest and most godless years of my life. I ignored the values I had been taught as a boy in church and embraced almost everything I knew in my heart to be wrong. I am ashamed to say that I was an agnostic during my college years.

> *"I command you: be strong and steadfast! Do not fear nor be dismayed, for the* LORD, *your God, is with you wherever you go."*
>
> JOSHUA 1:9

I graduated from the University of Georgia in 1989 with a degree in political science. Leaving college a few weeks after graduation was the best thing I could have done. I now see that God was watching over me during those hedonistic years and protecting me from harm. Many people have fond memories of their college experience, but I look back with a profound sense of sadness for the lost opportunities to take it more seriously and intense regret I feel for denying God during that time.

I am thankful that I grew up with faith-filled, hard-working parents who taught me the values I still live by to this day. Because of their strong influence and example, I have always been a hard worker and take my jobs very seriously. Immediately after graduation, I joined a large retail tire company in Atlanta and spent several years with this organization in roles of increasing leadership responsibility. On the outside I was making a good living and my career was going well, but I was empty inside. I threw myself into my job and left little time for a life outside of work. God was still nowhere to be found in my life, and attending church was the furthest thing from my mind. But God was still looking out for me. I met my future wife, Sandra, in 1993, and we dated and quickly fell in love. I was feeling truly happy for the first time in a decade and was able to shed the loneliness that had dogged me since my college days. We got engaged and were married in a Methodist church in November 1994 (since I was a non-practicing Baptist and she was a non-practicing Catholic, the Methodist church seemed like neutral territory for our wedding).

In October 1997, we were blessed with the birth of our first son. We were a very happy family, and everything seemed to be going according to plan. My career was progressing well in my new role as the vice president of recruiting for Waffle House, a billion-dollar restaurant company I had joined in 1995. My wife was able to leave her job and be a stay-at-home mother when our son was born. The challenge with this role was the time I spent away from my family and the heavy travel schedule. Determined to achieve a more balanced life, I changed the direction of my career in 1999 when I joined the leadership team of an Atlanta-based firm called Bell Oaks Executive Search. I was able to spend more quality time with my family, and the work was very rewarding. Being home for dinner every night was a nice change for the better!

Just when things seemed to be going well, the roof caved in. Our son had not been hitting the developmental milestones and was still not talking at age two. When he was twenty-seven months old, we received the diagnosis that our firstborn had autism. We were devastated. We both went into an emotional tailspin for a month as we tried to make sense of the diagnosis and understand how this could have happened. Many parents likely have an idealistic vision of what their lives should be like, but we never considered what it would mean to raise a child with special needs. I wish we had known how to pray back then, because we desperately needed God during those dark days.

"We are afflicted in every way, but not constrained; perplexed, but not driven to despair."

2 CORINTHIANS 4:8

We pulled ourselves together as we realized that this was not about us. It was about our son. He needed our love, our focus and the best medical care we could provide for him. As my wife and I were learning to give him what he needed, we began to talk more seriously about a church home. But still nothing happened. We desperately needed God, but we were lost and didn't know how to find him. (Today our oldest son is a teenager with high-functioning autism who attends a great school, makes good grades, and we are hopeful that he will attend college and lead as independent a life as possible.) Our second son was born in 2001. He is now a wonderful boy of eleven who is bright, active, and has developed as a typical child. He loves his brother very much and has a very compassionate heart, for which we are grateful. Both our children are incredible blessings, and we could not imagine life without them.

The years passed. My career continued to thrive. Attending church was an infrequent topic of discussion but nothing more. We decided to move from the extreme northern Atlanta suburbs in 2005 to get closer to my office and our older son's therapists. In the months leading to the move, my wife started talking to her old college roommate about the subject of faith and sought her guidance. Her friend is a devout Catholic and shared with my wife why she loved

Catholicism and what it would take for us to join the Church. God may have been sending us a message, because soon after we moved into our new home, my wife was driving around in the area, got lost and accidentally discovered St. Peter Chanel Catholic Church. When she came home, she excitedly told me about the beautiful parish and surrounding campus and her recent conversations with her friend, which led to a lengthy discussion about the possibility of us joining the Catholic Church. Sandra began asking around, talking to friends in the area and reading about the Church. While I was cautious about our becoming Catholic, I was very interested in its traditions and history, and I decided I should at least investigate. We met with the pastor, Father Frank McNamee, over the following weeks and were blessed to have so much time and guidance from this wonderful priest on what it meant to join the Church and our responsibilities to raise our children in the Catholic faith. We also learned much from him on our responsibilities to each other as a Catholic couple. In the fall of that year, we started attending Mass at St. Peter Chanel, and Sandra began formal instruction in the Rite of Christian Initiation for Adults (RCIA). She came into the Church at Easter of 2006. Our plan was for me to enroll in the next RCIA class so I could be with our sons while Sandra attended classes.

Then the Lord really got my attention. I was attending Mass with my family in early October 2005. The Mass had just begun and I felt very uneasy, a feeling that had started when I woke up that morning. I was as white as a sheet, sweating, trembling and felt very anxious. My family thought I was having a heart attack! This lasted about ten minutes. I remember thinking for the first time in my life, "Jesus, I don't know what to do anymore and I need your help. I surrender. Please lead...and I will follow." As soon as I thought these words, I felt something like a strong push from behind...then I felt absolutely fine. When we returned home from Mass and I shared the story with my wife, she skeptically asked me what I had done with her husband! I was suddenly on fire about joining the Church. As I surrendered control, the remaining obstacle around my heart had vanished. I met with a deacon of the parish the next day, and he helped me understand that I had been helped by the Holy Spirit to let go of twenty-three years of stubbornness, pride and ego that had been keeping me from Christ. At the age of forty, I had finally reached a place where I was ready to surrender to Christ and put his will before my own.

CHAPTER 2

Fruits of the Faith

On the Right Path

"So whoever is in Christ is a new creation:
the old things have passed away;
behold, new things have come."

2 CORINTHIANS 5:17

I HAD FINALLY SURRENDERED to Christ. What did he have in store for me? After my conversion and surrender that October, I was transformed from a reluctant and cautious investigator of the Church into a tireless student of the Truth I knew I had found. My spiritual awakening took my family and friends by surprise. As my wife was completing her return to the Church through RCIA, I kept busy with apologetics classes, Bible studies, reading, and talking to anyone I could about our Catholic faith to the point that I think I wore out our deacons and priests with my never-ending questions!

Our sons were baptized in 2006, and I started RCIA in early summer of that year. My wife and I had our marriage convalidated in November, and I came into the Church during the feast of Christ the King right after Thanksgiving. That year was such a turning point in our lives. God had blessed us with a great family, our faith had become an incredible source of strength, and we finally had the spiritual foundation that had always been missing in our lives. I will never forget that year, and I thank our heavenly Father every chance I get for not giving up on me and welcoming me home.

As I reflect on that time, I recognize that I experienced a "dying of self" when I acknowledged that I was no longer in charge of my life. It is amazing to me that I never felt stronger and more alive than at the very moment I chose to trust and surrender to his will. I had been in the spiritual wilderness for almost a quarter of a century, and Christ was bringing me home.

> *"The wind blows where it wills, and you can hear the sound it makes, but you do not know where it comes from or where it goes; so it is with everyone who is born of the Spirit."*
>
> JOHN 3:8

The last several years have been a wonder. I used to be all about work. Then I was committed to family and work. Now, the focus of my life is Christ first, then family, and work is third. The foundation is complete, and my heart has been permanently changed. By putting God's will clearly before my own, he has blessed our lives in so many ways, and my conversion has opened the door to an exciting future centered in Christ.

My business has thrived and I have been able to leverage my time to get involved with a number of non-profits that serve the Church and my community. In partnership with Dr. Phil Thompson of the Aquinas Center of Theology at Emory University and Deacon Mike Bickerstaff of St. Peter Chanel parish, I co-founded the annual Atlanta Catholic Business Conference in February 2009. I have been blessed to lead the St. Peter Chanel Faith at Work ministry, which is committed to helping Catholic men and women in the business and professional community integrate faith, family, and work into their lives. I have been a guardian in eucharistic adoration since January 2007, and it is always the best hour of my week. I started the Atlanta Chapter of the Woodstock Business Conference in 2007, which brings Catholic business leaders together monthly for Scripture discussion, dialogue about ethical and moral dilemmas at work, and strategies for becoming lights for Christ in the workplace.

My wife and I read constantly to more fully immerse ourselves in our faith. We pray faithfully and also pray with our children every night. I have always done business-related writing for my company, but since my conversion, the Holy Spirit has worked through me to write dozens of articles about my observations and challenges during the course of my faith journey, which hopefully will inspire others. I am also the senior editor for the popular Integrated Catholic Life eMagazine (www.integratedcatholiclife.org) which I co-founded with Deacon Mike Bickerstaff in early 2010. I jokingly tell people that my Baptist years as a young man have made me an evangelist for the Catholic Church today!

"So whoever is in Christ is a new creation: the old things have passed away; behold, new things have come."

2 CORINTHIANS 5:17

We still have challenges, and our lives are far from perfect. Our oldest son and his future are constant sources of concern, but we are comforted in knowing that we have asked God for his help and blessings, and that our son will find his way. Raising children in a world in which TV and the Internet can become surrogate parents is scary and requires vigilance and time to give our kids the love and direction they need. I struggle to give my wonderful wife all the support and love she needs from me. I am challenged with sometimes letting my will come before God's will, and I hope you will pray for me to have the humility to put my pride aside and let him lead me. God is in charge of the Hain family now, and after denying him for so long, I have been reconciled to him since that Mass in 2005, and I will never leave again.

Perhaps you can see my story like the prodigal son returning home, combined with Saul on the road to Damascus. I left Christ's embrace as a teenager; he never gave up on me while I lived in the spiritual desert, and I came back to him twenty-three years later.

He sent the Holy Spirit to get my attention in 2005, and I have been renewed in Christ since my conversion and surrender. I am hopeful that my life and my faith journey can in some way be an example for others to see that it is never too late to find the Truth and come home.

CHAPTER 3

Priorities

Priorities and a **Life Filled With Meaning**

"If everything is important, then nothing is important.
When it comes to living fuller, richer lives filled
with meaning, what are our true priorities?"

After surrendering to Christ and making the commitment to serve him, I recognized that I needed to make a new list of life priorities. It took me forty years to make my way into the Catholic Church, and I felt a burning desire to make up for lost time and maximize the second chance I had received. It was clear to me that things would never be the same, and my old compartmentalized life would no longer suffice. I had committed to putting Christ first in every area of my life, not just during Mass. The old work/life balancing act would need to give way to a new paradigm of Christ first, family second, and work third, with a focus on integrating faith, family, and work in a Christ-centered life filled with meaning.

We tend to make things more complicated than they really are. When it comes to priorities, many of us have checklists of some kind that include everything from going to the grocery store for milk to making sure our children get a great education. We confuse mundane tasks with what is truly important in life. If everything is important, then nothing is important. When it comes to living fuller, richer lives filled with meaning, what are our true priorities?

Since my conversion into the Catholic Church, I have thought and prayed a great deal about what is truly important and what Christ wants me to do. I tend to have a clear and unambiguous view of life, and the more I try to discern the Lord's plan and follow the new paradigm I laid out in the first paragraph of this chapter, the more apparent it becomes that I have just three simple priorities:

1. I will serve Christ and love him with all my heart.
2. My family is my primary vocation.
3. My workplace is also my ministry.

Seem like obvious choices? Perhaps. But, in my professional life and through the ministries I am involved in, I meet hundreds of people every year who have no priority list, desperately want a list but don't know where to start. Let's "unpack" each of these priorities and examine some of the specific actions we can take to help these priorities become reality for each of us in our pursuit of meaningful lives.

First priority: "I will serve Christ and love him with all my heart."

What does this mean? How do we serve Christ? If we love him with all our hearts, is there room for anything else? These are questions that are probably running through your mind. I would suggest that we serve and love him by being humble and obedient, by serving others, being good stewards, and surrendering to his will. Please consider these actions:

- **Daily surrender and ongoing conversion are necessary.** I learned early on in my faith journey that my surrender to God's will and subsequent conversion was not a one-time event. We must always put his will before our own and experience a "dying of self" so Christ can be in charge of our lives. I often find direction and inspiration in my favorite quote from Saint Ignatius of Loyola:

"Few souls understand what God would accomplish in them if they were to abandon themselves unreservedly to him and if they were to allow his grace to mold them accordingly."[1]

- **More time for prayer.** Would we give our family at least an hour of our time a day? Of course! So why not give the Lord an hour a day? It's not as difficult as we might think. Start the day with prayer. Before we check e-mail or read the morning paper, we can offer the day and our burdens up to God, thank him and ask for his forgiveness, help and blessing. We can pray the rosary in the car on the way to work and seek the intercession of our Blessed Mother. We can pray the Jesuit Daily Examen throughout the day. We should remember that prayer is any moment we turn our thoughts away from ourselves and toward God.

- **Become passionate about the Eucharist.** Want to fully experience Christ and be closer to him? Seek out the Real Presence of Christ in the Eucharist in daily Mass when possible and spend quiet time before the blessed sacrament in eucharistic adoration every week. As a former Protestant, I am quite familiar with the question: "Do you have a personal relationship with Jesus?" As a Catholic, I am incredibly grateful for the most personal and intimate union we can have with Christ when we receive him in the Eucharist.

- **Pursue joy, not happiness.** Father Luke Ballman, a past director of vocations for the Archdiocese of Atlanta, gave a wonderful talk at St. Peter Chanel a few years ago in which he described the pursuit of happiness as the "pursuit of the things of this world." We think we are seeking happiness in the bigger house, nicer car, better job, bigger paycheck...but do these things really bring happiness? His point was that all happiness must be preceded by joy and that all joy is Christ-inspired. Seek out and surrender your heart to Christ to find joy...and you will also find happiness.

- **Practice detachment.** Let's ask ourselves whether we really need "it," whatever "it" is. Let go of the material things that are in the way of our prayer lives, Mass attendance, charitable giving, volunteering and certainly our relationships with Christ. The catechism says, "Detachment from riches is necessary for entering the Kingdom of Heaven."[2]

Second priority: "My family is my primary vocation"

I have often written of the workaholic tendencies of the early part of my career that still plague me on occasion. When my first son was two years old, I began working for Bell Oaks Executive Search in the pursuit of a more balanced life. But it wasn't until my wife and I entered the Catholic Church that we truly understood our family is our number one vocation. Sounds great, but what does that mean? Aren't our careers our "vocations?" How do we accomplish this lofty goal? Here are a few practical steps we are focusing on to make this a reality:

- **Teach children about the faith and to love God.** Our children will love God and have strong faith only if we do. They will pray... if we do. They will be joyful about attending Mass...if we are. My wife and I try hard to be devout Catholics, and for us the greatest vocation is our family and raising our children to love and serve Christ and practice our Catholic faith.

- **Children need our time.** Let's put down the iPhone, turn off the television, cancel the golf outing, and spend more time with our kids. Quality time is the key. They need us actively engaged in talking or doing something with them...not reading a magazine while they watch *American Idol*. Also, dinnertime should be sacred. There is tremendous value in coming together for a family meal at least once a day. Also, I have always found car rides on the way to the kids' various activities to be a wonderful opportunity for conversations about whatever is on their minds.

- **Teach them responsibility and stewardship.** Helping our children learn responsibility at a young age and teaching them to have a good work ethic are great foundations for them to build upon as adults. Teaching them to serve and give back will help them be better human beings. This isn't classroom stuff. They will only learn from our example. Here is a helpful tip I will pass on from the Hain household: For the last five years we have asked our boys to each donate ten of their undamaged toys a few days before their birthdays and Christmas. We take them to our favorite charities and have them bring the toys inside for donation. They have learned that they must give...before they receive. (It also keeps the house a little cleaner!)

- **Love, love, love!** Showing our children we love them—and more importantly *telling* them we love them—is incredibly important. We hug our kids and tell them we love them every chance we get. But love is also caring enough to be tough, candid, and to provide limits. It is about loving each other. Want to give the kids a good example to follow? Show your spouse affection in words and deeds as often as possible. Remember: They will model the love we show in front of them.

Third priority: "My workplace is also my ministry."

Most of us spend the majority of our adult lives at work. The workplace today is a challenging environment in which to be open about our Christian beliefs. Political sensitivity and rigid company policies have led many of us to compartmentalize our faith in unhealthy and unnatural ways. I often hear people say, "I just leave my faith at the door when I get to work." But how can we possibly separate our spiritual selves from our physical being? In *Gaudium et Spes*, the

Second Vatican Council weighed in with this declaration: "This split between the faith which many profess and their daily lives deserves to be counted among the more serious errors of our age....The Christian who neglects his temporal duties, neglects his duties toward his neighbor and even God, and jeopardizes his eternal salvation. Christians should rather rejoice that, following the example of Christ Who worked as an artisan, they are free to give proper exercise to all their earthly activities and to their humane, domestic, professional, social and technical enterprises by gathering them into one vital synthesis with religious values, under whose supreme direction all things are harmonized unto God's glory."[3]

Here are some ideas and thoughts on how to practically carry your faith with you to work:

- **Be lights for Christ.** What does this mean? How can we do this? It rarely occurs to us to think about our own faith journeys, the examples we set for others and the Christ-inspired joy we radiate as the most effective ways to share our faith. Letting others see Jesus Christ at work in us is a powerful form of witness that will draw others to us who want what we have in their lives. Simple and authentic joy from us can often be the most effective way we share Christ and our beautiful Catholic faith with others.

- **Let love drive our actions.** *Agape*, the Greek word for selfless love, is the magic elixir that should drive our daily work activities. It is by acting in selfless and charitable ways toward others and putting their needs before our own that people will truly begin to see Christ in us. It is so easy to focus on our own desires and needs, but take up the challenge to make today about serving others. Even small acts of selfless kindness will have a dramatic impact on others. Chris Lowney, author of *Heroic Leadership*, wrote: "Love enables any company to welcome every sort of talent, irrespective of religion, race, social position, or credentials. Love is the joy of seeing team members succeed. Leaders motivated by love start from the premise that people will give their best when they work for those who provide genuine support and affection."[4]

- **Practice active stewardship.** Do you and your company give back to the community? 1 Peter 4:10 says: "As each one has received a gift, use it to serve one another as good stewards of God's varied grace." It is the right thing to do and resembles one who genuinely cares about the community. Get involved, make a difference and contribute. Perhaps if we lead, others will follow. Look for opportunities to reach out to the "Lazarus" in our lives today (from the parable of the rich man and Lazarus). Lazarus may be a depressed or troubled friend, a coworker who is dealing with personal tragedy or a homeless and hungry person on the street. Consider 1 John 3:17: "If someone who has worldly means sees a brother in need and refuses him compassion, how can the love of God remain in him?"

- **Show humility.** C.S. Lewis wrote in *Mere Christianity* that the greatest sin is pride, and the virtue that opposes pride is humility.[5] 1 Peter 5:5 says: "Likewise, you younger members, be subject to the presbyters. And all of you, clothe yourselves with humility in your dealings with one another, for: 'God opposes the proud but bestows favor on the humble.'" Humility is a vitally important characteristic for Christians. Humility means reflecting on our motivations for our actions and letting go of the outcome. We can enjoy the experience of life and not be obsessed with expectations others have of us or that we have of ourselves. Humility is trusting the work of the Holy Spirit. It is recognizing and being able to articulate our deepest desires for ourselves. When we are self-aware, we can find ways for self-expression...and know when to alter our behavior and actions to be more appreciative of our friends and coworkers. Luke 14:11 says, "For everyone who exalts himself shall be humbled, but the one who humbles himself will be exalted."

My intent in sharing these priorities is to show how simply we can alter our lives in ways that assimilate faith, family, and work, and put us on the path to a Christ-centered life, filled with meaning. Since my conversion, I have tried every day to live the actions I have shared and I assure you that I struggle like anyone else. The challenge, I believe, is to practice them not as a bunch of new "to-dos," but as part of a broader, unifying approach to a balanced and meaningful life that places Christ *first* in all areas of our lives.

We are faced with the choice between a compartmentalized life or an integrated life in which faith, family, and work are unified and centered in Christ. We are asked to "change our hearts," let go of our attachments to material things and place him first in our lives. We are challenged to know our moral non-negotiables and not cross ethical boundaries. We are asked to let others see Jesus within us and to share our joy with others. Our humble and virtuous example to others throughout the day will positively influence their behavior and individual faith journeys. An active prayer life—one that turns our day into a conversation with God and firmly places his desires before our own—will open us up to receive boundless grace.

My hope is for everyone to experience a true "conversion of the soul" and lead an integrated, balanced, and meaningful life. It isn't easy, but it is worth the journey. I encourage all of us to begin tomorrow with a firm disposition to do good, practice virtue, and emulate Christ. Constantly thank God and praise his name. Say a prayer to our Lord on the way to work or when we drop off the kids at school, asking for guidance and grace throughout the day. Be kind to people we meet and offer assistance freely without an expectation of return. Pray for Christ to show us that the challenges that present themselves each day are opportunities to grow in holiness and virtue.

I would like to close this chapter with a relevant quote from one of my favorite writers, Francis Fernandez, and his wonderful series of books *In Conversation with God*: "We have to show everyone that Christ is still alive by living heroically the events of our daily lives.

The apostolic vocation that we all received at baptism means giving witness in word and deed to the life and teaching of Christ. People said of the early Christians, "See how they love one another!" The pagans were really edified by this behavior and those who conducted themselves in this way had favor with all the people, as the Acts of the Apostles tells us.

"Normally Our Lord asks us to give a Christian witness through our ordinary lives, engaged in the same ways of earning a living, tackling the same concerns as other folk. We have to act in such a way that others will be able to say, when they meet us: 'This man is a Christian, because he does not hate, because he is ready to understand, because he is not a fanatic, because he is willing to make sacrifices, because he shows that he is a man of peace, because he knows how to love.'"[6]

I don't pretend to have all the answers. I have been particularly challenged in my life, especially with consistently living up to the third priority. There have been clear tradeoffs over the years in order to keep these priorities in order, and I anticipate more sacrifices in the future. My sincere hope is that somewhere in the thoughts and ideas I have shared in this chapter you will find the encouragement and inspiration necessary make a new priority list and commit to a Christ-centered life filled with meaning.

CHAPTER 4

Why Become Catholic?

A Journey **Toward the Truth**

"All that compelled me toward Rome can be understood as a growing conviction of the Truth of the Church and its inherent beauty."

IN THE FIRST three chapters I shared my surrender and conversion and explored a shift in life priorities, but a big unanswered question is simply: Why did I become a Catholic? As much as I love my wife and children, they were not the main reason. Was it a midlife crisis? No, turning forty can be traumatic, but that wasn't it. I ultimately joined the Catholic Church because I was seeking the Truth, even though I didn't realize I was on such a journey at the time. From that early summer of 2005 when the idea of considering the Catholic Church was first suggested, I have been drawn to the history and tradition of the Church. The early Church Fathers and their writings have had a profound effect on me. Growing up as a Southern Baptist, I was never exposed to the clear fact that the Eucharist was always at the center of worship from the early days of the Church or to the primacy of the Bishop of Rome. I have also learned that being Catholic is much more than knowing the catechism, the Bible, attending Mass, and memorizing important prayers. It is a living Church, with more than two millennia of history and tradition, that possesses the four marks of the True Church founded by Christ: it is one, holy, catholic, and apostolic. In the Catholic Church, I have the fullness of the faith that no other religion can claim or offer.

The Catholic Church is not only the Truth, it is also beautiful. The beauty of our faith is revealed through its sacraments, prayers and devotions, holy Mass, art, music, architecture, and the mysteries of the Eucharist. All that compelled me toward Rome can be understood as a growing conviction of the Truth of the Church and its inherent beauty.

The search for Truth can begin in many different places. I came from a place of deep appreciation of the Bible as the word of God when I was a teenager. As I grew older, I began to doubt the authenticity of the church I was attending. My doubting and teenage rebellion eventually left me spiritually arid for twenty-three years, as I explained in chapter one. When I began exploring Catholicism in the summer of 2005, I drew comparisons to what I had learned as a boy. How could these Protestant churches proclaim the Bible as the ultimate authority and yet reject the explicit teaching of Jesus on the Eucharist in John 6? How could I read Jesus' prayer for unity in John 17 and not wince as I considered that we were part of 30,000 Protestant denominations all claiming to "do things the Bible way?" How could I ignore the fact that many of our fellow Christians held opposing viewpoints and all used the Bible to justify their positions? Also, I thought, didn't the Truth exist prior to my Reformation-birthed denomination? If so, where was it now?

As I dug deeper into my research, I began to long for consistency, unity, and authority rooted in Truth, which was deeper and more historical than what I experienced as a youth. This period of study, countless conversations with priests and deacons in our community, and the subtle guidance of the Holy Spirit eventually led me to the Truth of Catholicism. Consider the clarifying words of *Lumen Gentium*: "This is the one Church of Christ which in the Creed is professed as one, holy, catholic, and apostolic, which our Savior, after his resurrection, commissioned Peter to shepherd, and him and the other apostles to extend and direct with authority, which he erected for all ages as 'the pillar and mainstay of the truth.'"[7]

Is my experience different because I am a convert? I think most converts would say being Catholic is a privilege. There is an almost palpable sense of excitement and enthusiasm about our newly discovered faith. It is as if one's life is completed, made whole by the experience of becoming Catholic. Many things I was struggling to understand began to make sense in light of the Church's teaching. I wonder if part of the reason for this is many converts I know perceive joining the Church as a wonderful gift at the end of a long journey in search of the Truth. Yet I have been puzzled to discover that a fair number of Catholics do not share this enthusiasm or experience. It seems they have lost touch with what is special about being Catholic. The faith of their youth or somewhat distant conversion has turned into a passive Catholicism in their adult years.

Fortunately, there are many lifelong Catholics whom I admire, respect, and appreciate for their deep-seated faith and love of the Church, and many of them are my mentors. I have learned from their experience and wisdom and owe them my love and gratitude.

Still, I ask myself why the Catholic Church attracts thousands of new converts each year and yet also has thousands leaving the Church each year. And why don't all Catholics feel the joy and passion that we converts feel in our practice of the faith? We long to be able to share our "discovery" and our excitement about the Church with those for whom the Church is already "home." With the guidance of the Holy Spirit, I continue to hope that my message provides help and inspiration to *all* Catholics: converts, lifelong Catholics, and reverts alike, who are seeking to more fully embrace their faith.

One of the key reasons that some of us may not fully appreciate the gift of our Catholic faith is familiarity. Years of familiarity with the culture of the Church may actually begin to breed apathy. Many of us are indeed proud to be Catholic but may see our faith as more of a passive rather than a dynamic part of our identities. Maybe we have taken all the classes, know the Catholic lexicon, and know the ins and outs of the Church. But in the midst of all this formal training or experience, is it possible we have missed the life-changing power of the gospel?

When familiarity hardens into apathy, it is not uncommon to look for something new and exciting or different to break the perceived monotony. One way this manifests itself is the move toward relativism. This move reduces the role of Truth in one's life and elevates the idea that ultimate Truth is the truth that "works for me." This leads to "cafeteria Catholicism," a description used by author and convert Dr. Peter Kreeft to describe those who mistakenly believe you can be an authentic Catholic and also live in opposition to the teachings of the Church.

I fully accept the teachings of the magisterium, but I realize that my full understanding of these teachings is a journey that may take me a lifetime to complete. When we begin to doubt the Church's teachings, we become susceptible to the influence of other "churches." If you can question one thing, you may soon question everything. This counterproductive pursuit will only take us further from Christ and the Church he founded.

> *"Whoever listens to you listens to me. Whoever rejects you rejects me. And whoever rejects me rejects the one who sent me"*
> LUKE 10:16

Another reason some of us may not fully appreciate and embrace our Catholic faith is a lack of sound knowledge and understanding of what Christ is teaching through his Church. It is hard for people to defend or even fully understand their faith unless they take the time to study it. "Therefore, from the day we heard this, we do not cease praying for you and asking that you may be filled with the knowledge of his will through all spiritual wisdom and understanding to live in a manner worthy of the Lord, so as to be fully pleasing, in every good work bearing fruit and growing in the knowledge of God" (Colossians 1:9–10).

One of the greatest pieces of advice I received early in my journey of faith is to stop, reflect and ask myself these questions on occasion: Am I lukewarm in my faith? What am I missing in my life? Do I have questions that need to be answered? Do I want to more fully appreciate my faith and don't know how? Is God truly first in my life, or is he competing for a share of my time? Am I ready to make a firm commitment to change my heart and my mind about how I view the Church and get back on the right path? What is God calling me to do? I often pray and reflect on my answers to these questions, and the process helps me stay on track. As a convert, I have also found the following habits to be enormously helpful in my faith journey. Hopefully, these will be helpful for you as well.

- **Vibrant prayer.** All of us need to take our burdens and questions to the Lord in prayer to seek guidance and answers. Start and end every day in prayer. We can spend time in adoration before the blessed sacrament, pray the rosary, do the Jesuit Daily Examen, pray the Divine Mercy Chaplet, meditate on Scripture, etc. I have learned from my own experience that a vibrant prayer life is essential to a vibrant faith life.

- **Surrender and convert daily.** I learned early on in my journey into the Church that my surrender to God's will and ultimate conversion was not a one-time event. I must always put his will before my own and experience a "dying of self" in order for Christ to be in charge of my life.

- **Accept and study the faith.** As I stated earlier, accepting the teachings of our Church is necessary, but so is the knowledge that my full understanding will take time. Trust that two millennia of Church teaching is much more reliable than what you or I might conjure up on our own. Go to a parish Bible study, take apologetics classes, read the Bible and catechism. Read great Catholic authors such as Dr. Peter Kreeft, Dr. Don DeMarco, Scott Hahn, Father Robert Barron, G.K. Chesterton, Dr. Edward Sri, Pope Benedict XVI, and Blessed John Paul II. Understanding our faith enables us to defend it to others.

- **Actively practice the faith.** Go to frequent reconciliation, attend daily Mass, frequently go before the blessed sacrament in adoration, observe all holy days, participate in the sacraments, and make sure your family is doing the same. Defend all life, from conception to natural death. Act with love toward all, as Christ taught us.

- **Privileged, not entitled.** We are all privileged to be part of the body of Christ in the Catholic Church, but privileges are earned, not granted. It requires dedication, obedience and practice. We must work to earn this privilege and to fully understand the gifts we have been given as Catholics.

All of us can benefit from considering where we are on our faith journeys and reflecting on the Truth and beauty of the Church. In today's world, I am grateful that Church teaching is clear and uncompromising, and this is one of the components I find most attractive about our faith. In the early days of my conversion, the attraction to the Truth and the work of the Holy Spirit drew me into the Church and my surrender to Christ. Today the desire for Truth drives me forward in my journey as I continue to grow in my faith.

Part Two

IT WAS *a* LOT *to* TAKE IN…

CHAPTER 5

Reconciliation

Getting Rid of Excess Baggage

*"Sin has weight. Every sin I commit in thought,
word, or deed is transformed into baggage
I carry around with me."*

ONE OF THE WONDERFUL GIFTS we have as Catholics is the sacrament of reconciliation. When I was studying Catholicism in 2005 prior to my conversion into the Church a year later, I was immediately drawn to this sacrament. I clearly understood through my studies that Christ had given his disciples the power to absolve sins, and our priests are the delegates of Christ and the successors of early disciples. If you ask Catholic converts about the first time they participated in reconciliation, don't be surprised at how deep and profound the experience was for them. I made my first reconciliation as a forty-year-old, and the experience of confessing decades of sin was both terrifying and cathartic for me. I will never forget how much better and liberated I felt when I cast aside the burdens I had been carrying around for all those years and the slate was wiped clean!

I have been thinking a great deal about one particular experience I had in reconciliation. I remember feeling an intense and unexplainable urge to go and confess my sins when I woke up that Saturday morning. I try to go every six weeks or so, but this was no routine visit to the priest for me. I needed to unburden myself of the numerous venial sins I had committed since I last participated in this sacrament. For possibly the first time in the years since I joined the Church, I was able to see the true nature of these sins as a tremendous burden on my shoulders, as a fog that kept me from seeing the path ahead, and absolutely as an obstacle in my relationship with Christ. I know these observations to be true because the moment I left the confessional booth I felt as though a huge weight had been lifted, my spiritual vision was restored, and I was again focused on serving the Lord.

Sin has weight. Every sin I commit in thought, word, or deed is transformed into baggage I carry around with me. As the weight accumulates, I begin to experience dryness in my prayer life. I make excuses for not reading the Bible and books on Catholic faith. My enthusiasm for sharing my faith with others becomes dampened under the burden of the sins I am carrying. My relationship with Christ is negatively affected, and the joy I should feel gives way to nagging self-doubt and guilt, all because of sin. I am ashamed to admit that I feel like I am going through the motions at times when the weight of sin becomes too great. These bad habits that creep in are my warning signs, but do I heed these warnings fast enough? How do I break out of this negative pattern?

Stop and reflect with me for just a minute. When is the last time you went to reconciliation? How did you feel the very moment you were absolved from your sins and performed your penance? Compare that feeling with your state of mind today. Have you noticed any of the warning signs I just mentioned? Any that I did not mention? These questions are not designed to make you feel guilty. I just want to encourage you to pause and reflect a little, as I have recently, on how accumulated sin throws us off track and creates barriers to our serving Christ.

It is easy for us to simply say: "I will go to reconciliation more often!" It is certainly desirable for us to participate in this sacrament more frequently, but I want to encourage all of us to think carefully about the real lesson of this chapter: Our sins, if not addressed and confessed, will negatively impact our relationship with Christ and the daily practice of our Catholic faith. The other lesson is to avoid destructive patterns: reconciliation, followed by a period of sins, reconciliation, followed by a period of the same sins....It is madness! How do we grow in our faith journey and break this pattern? Please consider these practical actions to lessen the burden of sin, break out of harmful routines and make the sacrament of reconciliation more fruitful:

- **Ask for help and guidance.** Don't go it alone. Ask our Lord for help. Give up your burdens to him in prayer. Fight through the "dry patches" in prayer and keep seeking him out. He is listening and is always ready to help. All he asks from us is our total surrender to his divine will. Just don't ask him to validate decisions we have already made.

- **Take time each day to review our actions.** Where did you sin? What caused it? How can you correct your behavior? Carry a reflection book for guidance. The Jesuit Daily Examen is a big help, but I also carry around a copy of the *Examination of Conscience* to review on occasion.

- **Look for patterns and repetition.** Which sins are you repeating? Consider who you are with and the environments you are in when we commit these sins. We can often break out of bad cycles by avoiding people and situations that trigger sin. I am not always successful at recognizing and changing these patterns, but when I do I feel that I am experiencing significant spiritual growth. The late Father John A. Hardon, SJ, once wrote: "Another word for bad habits is 'vices.' These bad habits are acquired by the repetition of bad actions. We may have the habit of unkind words, or of selfish behavior, which may have taken years to acquire. On the natural level, it would take years to change these bad habits into the opposite virtues. But with the grace of the sacrament of confession, we can overcome these vices in record time, beyond all human expectation."[8]

- **Know the enemy.** The prince of this world is the devil, and he will never, ever cease to try to trap us, sow seeds of doubt, and lead us astray. Our best defense against him is staying as close to Christ as possible in prayer and through the Eucharist. A pure heart, free of sin and cleansed through the sacrament of reconciliation pulls us toward Christ and keeps the enemy at bay. Saint Alphonsus Liguori wrote: "The devil does not bring sinners to hell with their eyes open: he first blinds them with the malice of their own sins. Before we fall into sin, the enemy labors to blind us, that we may not see the evil we do and the ruin we bring upon ourselves by offending God. After we commit sin, he seeks to make us dumb, that, through shame, we may conceal our guilt in confession."[9]

- **Be completely open and honest with your confessors.** Be sure to do a thorough examination of conscience and tell the priest everything. We can't expect to be absolved if we don't share with candor what we have done or failed to do. Also, we need to seek guidance on preventing sin as well as the absolution of sin, and our priests are here to help us. "When he celebrates the sacrament of penance, the priest is fulfilling the ministry of the Good Shepherd who seeks the lost sheep, of the Good Samaritan who binds up wounds, of the Father who awaits the prodigal son and welcomes him on his return, and of the just and impartial judge whose judgment is both just and merciful. The priest is the sign and the instrument of God's merciful love for the sinner."[10]

- **Trust in God's mercy.** We serve a merciful and loving God who is always ready to forgive us. Trust and have courage that our heavenly Father only wants what is best for you. Coming from my old compartmentalized life, learning to trust has been difficult. But, as with so many other lessons on my faith journey, I have been amply rewarded when I place my trust and faith in his infinite mercy. "Those who approach the sacrament of penance obtain pardon from God's mercy for the offense committed against him, and are, at the same time, reconciled with the Church which they have wounded by their sins and which by charity, by example, and by prayer labors for their conversion."[11]

I once heard Dr. Peter Kreeft say in a talk that the Church is "not a museum for saints" but "a hospital for sinners."[12] We all sin and fall short. Let's be mindful that these sins are a weight around our necks, they obscure our vision, and are obstacles to our relationship with Christ. Going to reconciliation more frequently is a great step, but consider the opportunities to shed this burden through increased self-awareness, different actions, deeper reflection, a stronger prayer life, and a sincere trust in the mercy of God. Leading faithful Catholic lives centered in Christ is challenging enough. Maybe, just maybe, we can stop tripping ourselves up along the way.

CHAPTER 6
Evangelization

The Fortress

*"If we only share our faith and witness with
other Catholics or worse, keep it to ourselves,
how will the Church grow and spread
Christ's message of love?"*

WHEN I ENVISION a fortress, it invokes thoughts of strength, security, and protection. The image is comforting, particularly when used in relation to one's faith. I recall speaking with someone I met in the early days of my conversion about my faith and discovered that he was also Catholic. After hearing my story, he explained to me the role faith played in his life. He described it as a fortress in that it made him feel safe and served as the foundation of his life. After a little probing I discovered that he was generally very quiet about his beliefs, and the thought of sharing Christ's message with others was daunting and uncomfortable. Before my very eyes, the safe and foundational fortress of faith he described was transformed into a fortress mentality.

His reserve and discomfort were understandable, and I recognize that not everyone is comfortable sharing his or her faith. But is this behavior not contrary to Scripture and the teachings of the Church regarding the call to evangelization? Are we sometimes hiding within "faith fortresses" of our own making?

Like many, I sometimes struggle with sharing my faith. I am writing this not to render judgment but to hopefully inspire all of us to think differently, change our behavior, and be Lights for Christ. One only has to read the Great Commission given to us by Jesus Christ himself in Matthew 28:19–20 to understand our expected role: "Go, therefore, and make disciples of all nations, baptizing them in the name of the Father, and of the Son, and of the holy Spirit, teaching them to observe all that I have commanded you. And behold, I am with you always, until the end of the age." Our Lord also calls us to evangelization in Matthew 9:37–38: "Then he said to his disciples, 'The harvest is abundant but the laborers are few; so ask the master of the harvest to send out laborers for his harvest.'"

I choose to believe that all of us mean well and have good intentions when it comes to bearing witness for Christ, but there are obstacles (many of our own making) that keep us from doing so. What are some of these and how can they be overcome?

- **I don't know what to say.** This advice has been attributed to Saint Francis of Assisi, "Preach the gospel at all times; use words if necessary." It is through the love and charity we give others and our daily example of Christ's love within us that allows us to bear witness. If we are truly Lights for Christ, people will be drawn to us, and the Holy Spirit will work through us. If necessary, the words will come.

- **I am not secure enough in my faith to witness to others.** We are not perfect. Only God is perfect. We can wait our entire lives to be prepared and worthy to evangelize and we will have wasted a lifetime of opportunity. Don't let our pursuit of sainthood keep us from sharing Christ's message with other potential saints.

- **I am not comfortable sharing anything personal, especially about my faith.** Transparency invites transparency! We can't expect someone to open up to us unless we are willing to do the same. Our faith journeys are a blessing, meant to be shared, and the witness we give may have a profound influence on someone desperately needing to hear the message. "One night in a vision the Lord said to Paul, 'Do not be afraid. Go on speaking, and do not be silent, for I am with you. No one will attack and harm you, for I have many people in this city" (Acts 18:9–10). Ask a new convert or someone experiencing a spiritual renewal how he reached this point on his faith journey. He will likely credit the Holy Spirit and name someone who reached beyond his comfort zone to share Christ's message. Let's try viewing ourselves as a channel through which the Holy Spirit can use our witness to connect with others.

- **I don't want to appear judgmental.** So don't judge. It's not your place. Our mission is to spread Christ's message of love and mercy, not tell people their sins. Pope Benedict XVI shares this guidance, "Nowadays, in a special way the world needs people capable of proclaiming and bearing witness to God who is love."[13] "The Church's mission is the extension of Christ's mission: to bring God's love to all, proclaiming it with words and with the concrete testimony of charity."[14] The Holy Father is clearly saying that we must witness with love...God's love. Be encouraging, listen attentively, offer assistance, share Christ's message and— absolutely—pray. These are the actions of love that will allow us to effectively bear witness.

- **Isn't evangelization the responsibility of the priests and deacons in our parish?** Absolutely not. We are *all* called to go and make disciples (Matthew 28:19). Reflect on the words of Blessed John Paul II in his encyclical *Redemptoris Missio*: "No believer in Christ, no institution of the Church can avoid this supreme duty: to proclaim Christ to all peoples."[15] In *Lumen Gentium*, Vatican II specifically describes the mission of the lay faithful, "The lay apostolate, however, is a participation in the salvific mission of the Church itself. Through their baptism and confirmation all are commissioned to that apostolate by the Lord himself. Moreover, by the sacraments, and especially by the holy Eucharist, that charity toward God and man which is the soul of the apostolate is communicated and nourished. Now the laity are called in a special way to make the Church present and operative in those places and circumstances where only through them can it become the salt of the earth. Thus, every lay person, in virtue of the very gifts bestowed upon him, is at the same time a witness and a living instrument of the mission of the Church itself, 'according to the measure of Christ's bestowal.'"[16]

- **I don't want to alienate my friends or new people I meet.** There is a difference between preaching and judging versus loving and sharing. If people respond to the "hope you have" and the "joy within you," they will be curious and ask *you* questions. But, this will *not* work if we stay inside our fortress of faith. Consider this passage from *In Conversation with God* by Francis Fernandez, "Ordinarily our first obligation will be to direct our apostolic activity towards those whom God has placed near us, those with whom we are in frequent contact. We should be opportunely apostolic, presenting Christ's teaching in an attractive and heartwarming way. We will not attract anyone to the faith if we are rash and impetuous; we will if we are kind, patient, and loving."[17]

So I ask, do these obstacles resonate with you? I am personally challenged by these, but my commitment to evangelize and witness for Christ remains strong. Reflecting on the profound impact Christ has had on my life since my conversion makes me want to share my story with everyone I meet. All of us have been given an incredible gift—Christ's redeeming love! At times we are weak, we may stumble on our faith journey, and we are sinners, but we must remember to be grateful and joyful for the countless blessings we have been given. In fact, one of the easiest ways to evangelize to others is to be joyful. When we are happy in our faith, we inspire and encourage others and create opportunities to witness for Christ. People want to hear the Good News.

Consider the fortress illustration again. In order to evangelize, we need to operate outside the walls of our faith fortresses and stand next to the cross. Our Lord is seeking people, just like you and me, to do his will and share the Good News. Francis Fernandez shares additional insight from *In Conversation with God*, "Ours is an age when Christ needs men and women who are able to stand beside the cross, strong, daring, simple, hard workers, without any human respect when it comes to doing good; men and women who are cheerful, who have as the foundation of their lives prayer—a relationship with Jesus that is full of friendship."[18]

If we only share our faith and witness with other Catholics or worse, keep it to ourselves, how will the Church grow and spread Christ's message of love? Will we make the necessary commitments to heed the call of the Great Commission, other supporting Scripture, the leadership of the popes, Vatican II and the catechism? What are simple ways we can all evangelize and bear witness for Christ? Consider doing the following:

- **Be salt and light.** Be a joyful, forgiving and generous person; in your workplace, at home in the community and with friends. Next to prayer, this is the most effective thing you can do. Let Christ's love and the blessings he has given be apparent to others. They will want to know the source of your happiness and this will likely initiate a faith conversation. "You are the salt of the earth. But if salt loses its taste, with what can it be seasoned? It is no longer good for anything but to be thrown out and trampled underfoot. You are the light of the world. A city set on a mountain cannot be hidden. Just so, your light must shine before others, that they may see your good deeds and glorify your heavenly Father" (Matthew 5:13–14, 16).

- **Pray.** Pray for courage. Pray that the Holy Spirit will work through you. Pray for opportunities to bear witness. Pray that God will allow you to recognize opportunities for evangelization. Make the sign of the cross and pray grace before each meal (public and private), and say prayers as a family. Prayer is the key because it prepares both your heart and those of others for moments of truth and grace.

- **Keep your faith journey on track.** It would be hypocritical for us to share the message of Christ's love if we didn't believe it and live it. This means living our faith at home and teaching our children about the Church and Christ's love for them. Pray, attend Mass, go to reconciliation frequently, go to eucharistic adoration, observe the sacraments, study your faith, and be joyful Christians. These actions will prepare you to share with *sincerity* the impact Christ has in our lives.

- **Share your stories with others and give witness to the blessings of Jesus in your life.** As I suggested before, be transparent! If you feel uncomfortable asking others about their faith, why not share yours? They will most likely be moved by your example and be open in return.

- **Reach out to the Lazaruses in your life every day.** I discuss this at length in the next chapter, but remember that Lazarus is the poor man covered with sores at the gate of the rich man in Christ's parable related in Luke 16:19–31. Can you think of a greater witness for Christ than to emulate our Lord and help those most in need? Think of the sick, jobless, depressed, troubled people in your life and reach out to them. Volunteering in a parish-based ministry is one of the best ways to get involved and make a difference. As you help them through their troubles, the Holy Spirit can work through you to share God's message of love!

- **Share or give a book, CD, DVD, article, or homily related to the faith.** This is a wonderful act of kindness that will help someone grow spiritually and give ample opportunity for further discussion about Christ and his Church. An interesting perspective on this type of evangelization is that it creates a safe environment to begin a faith dialogue. Let your gift open the door for a rich and engaging conversation, then allow the Holy Spirit to take over.

The fortress mentality is a real issue for many of us, and we have to remain committed and diligent about living our faith beyond those walls. This chapter is focused on simple ways to witness, but there are countless other ways to bring people Christ's message including extending an invitation to Mass or a parish event. Whatever we do, God will bless us for heeding the call to evangelization.

Let's go deeper and reflect on this quote from Blessed John Paul II, who wrote in *Springtime of Evangelization*:

"Evangelization is the Church's effort to proclaim to everyone that God loves them, that he has given himself for them in Christ Jesus, and that he invites them to an unending life of happiness. Once this Gospel has been accepted as the 'good news.' it demands to be shared. All baptized Christians must commit themselves to evangelization, conscious that God is already at work in the mind and hearts of their listeners, just as he prompted the Ethiopian to ask for baptism when Philip told him 'the good news of Jesus' (Acts 8:35). Evangelization is thus a part of the great mystery of God's self-revelation to the world: it involves the human effort to preach the Gospel and the powerful work of the Holy Spirit in those who encounter its saving message. Since we are proclaiming a mystery, we are servants of a supernatural gift, which surpasses anything our human minds are fully grasping or explaining, yet which attracts by its inner logic and beauty."[19]

I am hopeful that this image of the fortress and its dual nature will encourage you to reflect on your approach to evangelization. We can either live securely inside our faith fortress or we can heed the call to evangelize and operate outside its walls. To those who faithfully practice evangelization the way our Lord intended, thank you for showing us the way by your example. As lay people, we can make a dramatic impact on the lives of so many individuals if we will only accept our responsibility to share the dramatic impact Christ has on our lives. Who will hear our stories today?

CHAPTER 7

Stewardship

Seeking **Lazarus**

*"Consider the possibility that in today's society
our problem is not that we don't see Lazarus.
We see him, accept his plight, and either
throw money at him or ignore him."*

AS I HAVE GROWN in my Catholic faith, I find this to be a difficult and complex topic: Being good stewards of God's blessings and truly helping those in need. Donating money to good causes is very important, but actually lifting the burdens of the Lazarus in our lives is even *more* essential. If you will recall Jesus' parable in Luke 16:19–31, Lazarus was a poor man covered with sores lying outside the door of a rich man. Lazarus would have been content with simply the scraps from his table, but the rich man did not take notice of Lazarus until it was too late. Then Lazarus was in heaven with Abraham while the rich man was tormented in hell.

Proverbs 21:13 says, "Those who shut their ears to the cry of the poor will themselves call out and not be answered." Let's prayerfully consider how we can return to basic human interaction with our brothers and sisters in Christ who are struggling and share not only through charitable giving, but also through love, prayer, witness, listening or even a warm embrace. Let's also expand our definition of Lazarus to include not only the countless poor, sick, homeless, and hungry of the world, but also more locally: the jobless neighbor, depressed coworker, sick relative, financially struggling friend or special needs child who attends school with your own. Lazarus is everywhere in our lives…if we have the courage to seek him.

Consider the possibility that in today's society our problem is not that we fail to see Lazarus. We see him, accept his plight, and either throw money at him or ignore him. I realize that sounds harsh, especially in light of most statistics that indicate Americans are generous to those in need. We obviously live in a financially generous country. The enormous sums of money that flow from individuals and corporations to good causes is *overwhelming*. So what is the problem? I recognize that many people generously give their time, talent, and treasure to good causes, and they are truly a blessing. But many of us may be hiding behind walls of our own creation from which we only dispense money to address the problems of the world or worse, *we do nothing at all.*

As I thought and prayed about this chapter, I recalled Christ's words in Matthew 25:35–46: "'For I was hungry and you gave me food, I was thirsty and you gave me drink, a stranger and you welcomed me, naked and you clothed me, ill and you cared for me, in prison and you visited me.' Then the righteous will answer him and say, 'Lord, when did we see you hungry and feed you, or thirsty and give you drink? When did we see you a stranger and welcome you, or naked and clothe you? When did we see you ill or in prison, and visit you?' And the king will say to them in reply, 'Amen, I say to you, whatever you did for one of these least brothers of mine, you did for me.' Then he will say to those on his left, 'Depart from me, you accursed, into the eternal fire prepared for the devil and his angels. For I was hungry and you gave me no food, I was thirsty and you gave me no drink, a stranger and you gave me no welcome, naked and you gave me no clothing, ill and in prison, and you did not care for me.' Then they will answer and say, 'Lord, when did we see you hungry or thirsty or a stranger or naked or ill or in prison, and not minister to your needs?' He will answer them, 'Amen, I say to you, what you did not do for one of these least ones, you did not do for me.' And these will go off to eternal punishment, but the righteous to eternal life."

This Scripture is the source of the Catholic Church's teaching on the Seven Corporal Works of Mercy, which have helped me more deeply understand our obligation, as instructed by Christ, to help the less fortunate. They are:

- To feed the hungry
- To give drink to the thirsty
- To clothe the naked
- To shelter the homeless
- To visit the sick
- To visit the imprisoned
- To bury the dead

Nowhere in the Scripture or this list do I see instructions to "write a check" or "donate online." I recently took stock of my own stewardship and was surprised and disappointed that most of what I do consists of raising money for charities, writing personal checks, and attending nonprofit board meetings. Less than a quarter of my time actually placed me in front of those who needed me. I care very much about the charities and groups I help, but I have allowed a wall to be formed around me that keeps me from the personal interaction needed to really make a difference. I know the money I raise and the influence I wield is important, but "showing up" and really ministering to the people in need is what is required. Using our expanded definition of Lazarus, I have countless opportunities around me on a daily basis to help others, but I own the responsibility to be more proactive and reach out.

"If a brother or sister has nothing to wear and has no food for the day, and one of you says to them, 'Go in peace, keep warm, and eat well,' but you do not give them the necessities of the body, what good is it?"

JAMES 2:15–16

If you reflect on the many references to almsgiving in Scripture, you must remember that in biblical times, people were most likely seeing, touching and talking directly with the people to whom they were giving alms and showing mercy. Today, however, the size of the world's population, the economic segregation within our cities, the distance between us and advances in technology often reduces our almsgiving and acts of mercy to a "point and click" exercise on the computer. I know full well that the counter-argument to this chapter will be: that I am negating the impact of financial giving and that there is not enough time to physically be present and reach out to others. *I strongly and respectfully disagree.* We are running the risk of losing our basic humanity if we continue to avoid the personal interaction I am advocating.

Again, donating money is very important, but showing up and lifting or sharing the burdens of the Lazaruses in our lives is even more important. My friend John Ruane, author of *Parish the Thought: An Inspirational Memoir of Growing Up Catholic in the 1960s,* gave me his thoughts on the struggles he faces with this issue, "We are all so busy dealing with our own schedules and problems that it has become very easy to walk by Lazarus without seeing him. I find it very easy to recognize and help Lazarus when he or she approaches me on the street asking for food or money. We get into our own pace in life. We have our own habits, our priorities and focus. I have got to get a hundred things done today. I just have to get them done. We are focused on our mission. Taking time to stop, step outside of our habits, our pace—to recognize and help Lazarus, is the new habit I am working to develop."

How do we reach beyond the cultural, emotional and spiritual walls we have created to show mercy to Lazarus as Christ intended? How do we meet our obligations to help our brothers and sisters in Christ? Are we overwhelmed by the world's problems or do we feel that they don't affect us? Is it uncomfortable to be vulnerable enough to admit the problem and act on it? Are we afraid that people will want more from us than we can give? Do we even know where to start? I struggle with these answers but humbly and prayerfully encourage everyone to embrace the following actions or ideas to help us develop the courage and commitment to change our attitude toward Lazarus and take action:

- **Ask our Lord for guidance.** Pray for the clarity of sight to see Lazarus all around. Pray for the courage to break free of the barriers we have created and help Lazarus. Pray for the Holy Spirit to guide your actions. I am grateful for this insight from Charlie Douglas, author of *Rich Where It Counts* and *Awaken the American Dream*, "Prayer today is so often about informing God of our wishes and our will. The truth is, however, that prayer is about conforming our will to God's. Jesus made this clear in the Garden of Gethsemane when he earnestly prayed that above all his Father's will be done. And part of our Father's will is to sacrificially carry our crosses in service to the homeless, the poor, the despondent and the unloved. To be the hands and feet of Christ to the Lazaruses all around us is a beautiful prayer."

- **Be present...and act today.** Watch, listen, and act. Look daily for the presence of Lazarus in your family, friends, coworkers, and strangers. Someone is struggling at this very moment with any number of personal ailments or challenges. In fact, a majority of our adult lives is spent at work, so your best opportunity to directly help others may be through your work colleagues. Ask the Holy Spirit to help discern who needs your help today. Don't wait until tomorrow because there may not be the same opportunity to reach out and make a difference in their lives.

- **Love our neighbors.** God is love. He loves everyone the same without prejudice. From Genesis 5:1–2 we know God created man in his own likeness. It is important to remember this as you regain your humanity through the loving generosity shown to fellow brothers and sisters in Christ. "Teacher, which commandment in the law is the greatest?' He said to him, 'You shall love the Lord, your God, with all your heart, with all your soul, and with all your mind. This is the greatest and the first commandment. The second is like it: You shall love your neighbor as yourself. The whole law and the prophets depend on these two commandments" (Matthew 22:36–40).

- **Practice and encourage generosity.** "Giving enlarges the heart and makes it youthful, with an ever greater capacity for loving. Selfishness, on the other hand, impoverishes the heart and narrows its horizons. The more we give, the richer we become" (Francis Fernandez, *In Conversation with God*, Vol. 1, page 192, Section 26.1). We must let the love for Jesus that we feel in our hearts be obvious to all we encounter. Forced giving or obligatory assistance to others is not pleasing to Christ and runs counter to his teachings.

- **Faith without works is dead.** Get involved by physically being there. There are countless ministries and charities that need help, not just money. Serving at soup kitchens, visiting the elderly, participating in prison ministry, volunteering with the Special Olympics, building homes and schools in Haiti....These are some of the countless opportunities available. My friend Glen Jackson, head of an Atlanta-based public-relations firm and a faithful servant of Christ, recently shared these thoughts with me: "In the Book of James in the New Testament, we read an often-quoted and discussed passage: 'For just as the body without the spirit is dead, so faith without works is dead.' This Scripture reminds us that as the body of Christ, we are to work—*really work*—for our Lord. We are to be men and women of action and joy because the Holy Spirit lives in us. But how should we work? James gives us the answer in a later passage when he says, 'Show by your good life that your works are done with gentleness born of wisdom.' It is the type of work that its recipients respect, appreciate and are touched by because of its unforced sincerity. *Now we can't do this by simply sending a check.* Our time on earth is a mist that appears for a little while and vanishes. So make the most of it. A prayer to help stay focused is: 'Lord, help me make a difference for you that is utterly disproportionate to who I am.' Amen to that, and let's press on and be about our work of advancing the kingdom with our time, talent, and treasure."

- **Practice detachment.** This may well be the hardest for us to accomplish: detaching ourselves from the pursuit of wealth for wealth's sake and putting more time and energy into our relationship with Christ and our commitment to helping others. Remember Lazarus and the rich man? The rich man's wealth and abundance blinded him to the plight of Lazarus. In the end he lost everything while Lazarus was comforted in heaven. Pope Benedict XVI wrote, "According to the teaching of the Gospel, we are not owners but rather administrators of the goods we possess: these, then, are not to be considered as our exclusive possession, but means through which the Lord calls each one of us to act as a steward of his providence for our neighbor. In the Gospel, Jesus explicitly admonishes the one who possesses and uses earthly riches only for self. In the face of the multitudes, who, lacking everything, suffer hunger, the words of Saint John acquire the tone of a ringing rebuke: 'If someone who has worldly means sees a brother in need and refuses him compassion, how can the love of God remain in him?' (1 John 3:17). In those countries whose population is majority Christian, the call to share is even more urgent, since their responsibility toward the many who suffer poverty and abandonment is even greater. To come to their aid is a duty of justice even prior to being an act of charity."[20]

- **Serve quietly.** We can't honestly provide aid to Lazarus and honor the Lord if the motivation is recognition and glory for ourselves. As Jesus said in Matthew 6:1–4, "[But] take care not to perform righteous deeds in order that people may see them; otherwise, you will have no recompense from your heavenly Father. When you give alms, do not blow a trumpet before you, as the hypocrites do in the synagogues and in the streets to win the praise of others. Amen, I say to you, they have received their reward. But when you give alms, do not let your left hand know what your right is doing, so that your almsgiving may be secret. And your Father who sees in secret will repay you."

It is a sad indictment of our times that the more perceived gain we see from technology and the pursuit of wealth, the more distant we are becoming from the less fortunate. I have explored the moral imperative for helping Lazarus, but we are also encouraged to do so through countless scriptural references to "blessings we will receive" and the "building up of treasure in heaven." Consider the simple and compelling Scripture references found in Proverbs 14:21: "Whoever despises the hungry comes up short, but happy the one who is kind to the poor!" and Proverbs 11:24–25: "One person is lavish yet grows still richer; another is too sparing, yet is the poorer. Whoever confers benefits will be amply enriched, and whoever refreshes others will be refreshed."

God will show us the way if we only ask it and his pleasure is clear and unmistakable when we give freely of ourselves and our treasure to those in need. Jim Schippers, my friend and the founder of the St. Peter Chanel Business Association, shared with me a touching story about his encounter with a homeless person in downtown Atlanta and the struggles he had leading up to that encounter, "Let us be real with God....The more we are honest with God the greater our graces will be. I realize that is such a simple statement, but let me explain what I mean. I work in downtown Atlanta, and as I walk to and from work, and during my lunch break, I come across a number of homeless people. As I walk by each and every one of them, conflicts and reasons for not giving rise up within me. What will this person do with the money? I can't give to every 'beggar' that comes across my path, right? Or, I have left my wallet in the office, so no guilt there.... I have struggled with this, and interestingly enough as I pass by each homeless person, I find it difficult to look them in the eye. Yes, I have these excuses *per se*, and after much struggle and stubbornness on my part I asked Christ to help me. I gave to him my doubts, the whole lot of my feelings (good and bad) regarding this situation. A few nights later I was leaving a Braves game and a homeless person asked me for money. I looked him in the eye and gave him a dollar. He smiled, I smiled back, and peace entered my soul. It took a while for me to get there, but Christ was with me prodding me along the whole way, all I had to do was be honest with myself and ask for his graces."

In conclusion, I would again ask that we broaden our definition of Lazarus to include those people we see every day as well as the less fortunate in our community and around the world. Avoid the trap the rich man fell into, which cost him a life in torment. As another friend, Dr. Ron Young, observed, "Most of us are more like the rich man than the beggar, Lazarus. We have abundance, especially when compared to the rest of the world. There is so much we can do to reach out to those in need in our everyday lives, but unfortunately we can become so consumed with the trappings of success and relative prosperity (emotional and financial) that we fail to see the people who need us most."

I believe a majority of us want to help and that most of us are well-intended. Try to reflect at different points each day on your actions toward others and examine those missed opportunities to help someone who is struggling, so you can rectify them later. Expanded horizons and active engagement are required. Let's evolve our good intentions to a higher standard where we begin to recognize Lazarus more clearly and frequently and our first words are "please let me help you." Also, remember that we all have the potential to be Lazarus some day.

"There, but for the grace of God, go I."

CHAPTER 8
Ecumenical Outreach

They Know I'm Catholic, Right?

*"The Holy Spirit worked through me, a Catholic,
to reach these Protestant men in their church
on a Sunday morning."*

COMING FROM a Baptist background, you might think it would be easy for me to share my Catholic faith with Protestants. Think again. I gave a talk one Sunday morning to the men's club of a large Atlanta Methodist church at the request of an old friend. When he asked me to speak to this group months before the talk, I responded with a question that I would ask him repeatedly every time we got together: "They know I'm Catholic, right?" I engage one-on-one with people of other faiths almost every day and always enjoy the dialogue, but this was very different, as I would be going on their turf to deliver a talk. I let nagging self-doubt creep in and began to regret my commitment over the last few weeks leading up to the talk.

I speak to groups fairly often, and this should not have been a big deal, but speaking to a large group of Protestants was pushing me way out of my comfort zone. How would they respond? Would they ask me questions I couldn't answer? Would they start quoting Scripture and maligning the Church? What if they insulted the Blessed Mother? Would they criticize Pope Benedict? What would I do?!?!

My friend tried to reassure me with what he thought were encouraging words: "Don't worry; most of them are former Catholics." Good grief! Not only was I speaking as a Catholic in a Methodist church, but I was speaking to a group of former Catholics who had left the Church! How nice. It would be just my luck if everyone there had lingering issues they would love to take out on me. Then I had an epiphany a few days before I spoke and remembered three important things:

1. I needed to stop worrying and start praying. I needed to give up my fear and anxiety to the Lord, trust in him and ask for strength and the guidance of the Holy Spirit.
2. This was an unbelievable opportunity to share the joy of my Catholic faith with my Christian brothers, many of whom were once Catholic.
3. I know my friend, and he would not put me in a negative situation like the one my overactive imagination had cooked up. I needed to have faith and trust in our friendship and his good intentions. I needed to avoid giving in to unfair stereotyping, which I would resent if it were directed at me.

Before I share with you what happened at the talk, let's take a brief timeout and reflect a little on giving witness and ecumenical outreach. I just illustrated the fear and anxiety many Catholics feel about sharing their faith. I have heard countless times that we must be careful here in the "Protestant South." We may get questions about the Virgin Mary, or why we have priests hear our confessions or why we "pray to" saints. There is a fear that they could pounce on us by using Scripture to attack our beliefs. A fearful and insecure Catholic often becomes a quiet Catholic, but Jesus expects more from us. How will the Church grow and spread Christ's message of love if we only share our faith and witness with other Catholics or worse, keep it to ourselves? Matthew 9:37–38 says, "Then he said to his disciples, 'The harvest is abundant but the laborers are few; so ask the master of the harvest to send out laborers for his harvest.'"

In my professional life, I encounter new people every day. Since my conversion to the Church I have been very open and transparent with others about my faith. In all of my numerous encounters with people of different faith backgrounds, I have had very few negative experiences. I find people to be curious about Catholicism, not adversarial. I am not naïve, and I recognize there are people who have strong negative feelings toward the Church, but they may be having those out of misguided intentions, misunderstandings, or lack of knowledge. We have an opportunity during these encounters to explain our Catholic faith, dispel the rumors, and refute the myths. So many times in these conversations I have observed that we are more aligned than either of us realized and that often language and misunderstandings are the biggest barriers to agreement. But first we must know our Catholic faith before we can explain it to anyone else.

> *"Always be ready to give an explanation to anyone who asks you for a reason for your hope, but do it with gentleness and reverence, keeping your conscience clear, so that, when you are maligned, those who defame your good conduct in Christ may themselves be put to shame."*
>
> 1 Peter 3:15–16

Now, back to that talk at the Methodist church.

The prayers worked. The Lord gave me the peace and strength I needed. The group could not have been more kind or welcoming (is there a lesson here?). I actually felt very comfortable when I rose up to speak and trusted in the Holy Spirit to convey the right words. I started out by sharing my faith journey into the Church before launching into a talk titled "Priorities and a Life Filled With Meaning," in which I outlined my life priorities and the practical actions I was taking to ensure that I stayed on the right path. They heard quotes from saints and popes and lots of Scripture and catechism references. I hoped they would see me as a father and husband struggling with the same issues they struggle with, and how keeping my focus on serving Christ and putting him first in my life kept me on the right path. The audience applauded loudly when I finished, and many of them came up after to say that I really connected with them. They asked for a copy of the talk, which I was glad to provide to them. Many others asked if we could have coffee in the weeks ahead to discuss why I was so joyful about my Catholic faith, as they were eager to learn more.

I didn't do anything extraordinary, and I am not a particularly gifted speaker. The Holy Spirit worked through me, a Catholic, to reach these Protestant men in their church on a Sunday morning. Many of us will likely have numerous encounters in our lifetimes with people of different faiths. We are blessed as Catholics to possess the truth and the fullness of the faith. All it takes is our willingness to share our joy, a little courage, humility, transparency, and prayer to give a powerful witness for our Lord.

Are we willing to trust Jesus and allow him to work through us today?

CHAPTER 9

The Blessed Mother

Learning to Love **the Blessed Mother**

"I am inspired by the humility, strength, and discernment of a young teenage girl who said 'yes' to being the mother of Christ. Her answer, freely given, was arguably the most important 'yes' the world has ever known."

FOR YEARS I have had a strong desire to write about my ever-growing appreciation and love for the Blessed Mother. Growing up as a Baptist, leaving that church as a teenager and living in a spiritual wasteland until I experienced the significant personal conversion I described in chapter one, I never thought about Mary. Since joining the Catholic Church, I have gone through several phases in my feelings about her: mild curiosity, strong interest, education, revelation, appreciation... and now devotion and love.

What has brought about this change? How did Mary grow so significantly in my affections? Was it the death of my mother, Sandi, in 2010 that helped me draw closer to the Blessed Mother? The answer is complicated. I would love to tell you that it happened all at once in some miraculous epiphany. No, my experience has been much more gradual over the last few years, and as the phases above indicate, I had to educate myself on Mary before I knew how to love her. Today it is second nature for me to ask the Blessed Mother for her intercession and prayers, and the rosary has become an important part of my prayer life.

As we read about Mary in Scripture, the writings of the saints and early Church Fathers, our popes and more contemporary authors, we discover her vital role as the Mother of Christ, the Mother of his Church and the Mother of all humanity. Mary is the "New Eve," and it is natural that we love and revere her. It is also appropriate and expected that we should seek out the Blessed Mother in prayer to intercede for us with her son, Jesus Christ.

The more I read about Mary and draw closer to her in my prayers, I keep coming back to three essential lessons. They are apparent in every mention of Mary in the Bible and have been explored and taught by the Church for millennia. I am talking about surrender, service, and love.

Trustful Surrender to God's Will

I am inspired by the humility, strength, and discernment of a young teenage girl who said yes to being the mother of Christ. Her answer, freely given, was arguably the most important "yes" the world has ever known. She is the ultimate example of unconditional commitment to God's will. Our faith requires an ongoing surrender and conversion that is often difficult to conceive and even harder to do, yet we can learn from the Virgin Mary's lifelong example of placing God's will first in her life.

We are also called to respond to God's invitation, to say "yes" to a relationship with him. This is what Mary's fiat, "Let it be done to me," is all about. In saying "yes" to God, as Mary did, we are able to discover the path to conversion and enter into a close relationship with him. Every time I pray the rosary, I think of the annunciation and Mary's humble surrender, and I am both reminded and encouraged that I must let go of my pride, give up control, and surrender everything to him.

Generosity and Service

The Blessed Mother does not receive that many mentions in the gospels, but two of them refer specifically to her selfless desire to help and serve others. Her visit to her pregnant cousin Elizabeth when she herself was pregnant with Jesus speaks volumes about her generosity and desire to serve. We receive the scriptural basis for the Hail Mary in Elizabeth's timeless greeting of Mary in Luke 1:41–43: "When Elizabeth heard Mary's greeting, the infant leaped in her womb, and Elizabeth, filled with the Holy Spirit, cried out in a loud voice and said, 'Most blessed are you among women, and blessed is the fruit of your womb. And how does this happen to me, that the mother of my Lord should come to me?'"

The second scriptural reference to Mary's generosity is at the wedding of Cana in John 2:1–11. Her concern over the needs of the wedding guests and the lack of wine caused her to ask her son to help. He performs the first of his public miracles at the request of his mother and begins his public ministry. This is also a clear statement about Mary's role as intercessor.

We can't ignore the clear and obvious focus of her entire life—from the time of the annunciation to the assumption—was an outpouring of generosity and service as she put aside all of her personal plans and desires to do God's will. Can we learn from Mary's example? Where can we show generosity and selfless service in our lives today?

Love and Devotion

The Blessed Mother spent her entire life lovingly devoted to our Lord. She loved him as her son and loved him as the Savior of humanity. Mary also loves each of us...her children. At the foot of the cross, Mary was clearly identified as the Mother of mankind as we read in John 19:26–27: "When Jesus saw his mother and the disciple there whom he loved, he said to his mother, 'Woman, behold, your son.' Then he said to the disciple, 'Behold, your mother.' And from that hour the disciple took her into his home." Mary's pure love for her son, Jesus Christ, and her love for all of us is a wonderful example we should follow. Our prayers to the Blessed Mother help us obtain the graces we require through her intercession with our Lord and ultimately we draw closer to him through that intercession. As I reflect during my rosary or at other times when I am thinking about Mary, I am inspired to show more love toward others and deepen my devotion to my own family, friends, and the Church.

One of the reasons I have waited so long to write about our Blessed Mother is my insecurity about my knowledge of her. I am not a theologian, and fully understanding the many aspects of Church teachings about Mary's life is a little daunting. But the truth is very few of us are theologians and we need to do the best we can to understand the role of Mary in our lives through prayer, reflection and reading. One of the best ways I know to deepen our understanding of (and connection to) Mary is to faithfully pray the rosary...every day if possible. Saying the prayers, reflecting on the mysteries and asking for her intercession has been a blessing for me and a real source of comfort and peace.

I don't know how you feel about Mary. You may have a growing reverence and love for her or you may mumble and rush through saying the Hail Mary. Wherever you are, I encourage you to learn more about the Blessed Mother, go to her often in prayer, ask for her holy intercession with her Son and simply...love her. My faith has grown over the last few years in part because my love for Mary has grown as well.

Blessed John Paul II once said, "From Mary we learn to surrender to God's will in all things. From Mary we learn to trust even when all hope seems gone. From Mary we learn to love Christ, her Son and the Son of God."[21] This is a beautiful and eloquent summation of the powerful role the Blessed Mother plays in our faith and our relationship with her Son, Jesus Christ.

Memorare

"Remember, O most gracious Virgin Mary, that never was it known that anyone who fled to thy protection, implored thy help or sought thy intercession, was left unaided. Inspired with this confidence, I fly unto thee, O Virgin of virgins my Mother; to thee do I come, before thee I stand, sinful and sorrowful; O Mother of the Word Incarnate, despise not my petitions, but in thy clemency hear and answer me. Amen."

CHAPTER 10

The Saints

Lessons From
Saints Peter, Paul, Joseph, and Augustine

"I am an unworthy sinner, but I know that I must strive every day to become a saint. A life focused on anything less would be a tragedy."

●

LEARNING ABOUT the communion of saints and their role in the Church was not as difficult for me to grasp as many might believe. The concept of praying for others is very common in Protestant churches. Catholic devotion to the saints is nothing more than admiration and respect for the memory of the dead heroes of the Church who chose to surrender their will and often their lives to serve God and his Church. What sets the saints apart is that they were ordinary human beings like you and me who were extraordinarily faithful to God, and their lives serve as role models for us. All of us are called to lead lives of holiness and become saints. The examples and faith of these courageous men and women can show us the way.

As I reflect on the role the saints have played in my faith journey, four saints stand out as ones I can relate to best. Saints Peter, Paul, Joseph, and Augustine have had the most meaningful, profound influence on my life so far. I have prayed to ask many of the saints for their intercessions, but I keep coming back to these remarkable men and the lessons they have taught me through the examples of their lives.

Saint Peter

I can absolutely relate to a man with a temper who often sticks his foot in his mouth! What I most connect with about Saint Peter is that he represents all of us in our frailties, imperfections, and inclination to sin. He denied Jesus three times and yet he was given the keys to the kingdom. He was not perfect, but he was forgiven by our Lord and became the first pope.

My shortcomings have paralleled those of Saint Peter in numerous ways, but there is hope for me in his example of persistent efforts to serve Jesus despite his failings, and the fact that our Lord is always willing to forget the past and show forgiveness.

Saint Paul

I don't know whether I would consider myself a missionary, but my passion for sharing our Catholic faith has been heavily influenced by this apostle and his extraordinary life. Like Saint Paul, I came from a background that seemed poorly suited for the kind of life I try to lead today. He was a Jewish zealot who persecuted Christians. I was a former Baptist who spent twenty-three years hiding from God and avoiding any kind of faith. Just as he went through a powerful personal conversion on the road to Damascus, I went through a similar experience in the Mass I referred to in chapter one when I surrendered to Christ and made the commitment to serve him. Much of what we know about Saint Paul comes from his letters to the fledgling Christian communities he helped found in the books of the New Testament. In my own small way, I have tried to reach others through my writing, and I am always inspired by the sacrifice, suffering, and faithfulness of the Apostle to the gentiles.

Saint Joseph

As a father and husband, who better for me to emulate than Saint Joseph? I have long been drawn to my patron saint and find in his quiet example the encouragement to be more courageous, trusting, and faithful in God's promises. As the father of a son with special needs, I often feel hard-pressed to give my oldest son the love and patience he needs from me. I frequently feel inadequate when I advise and guide my younger son through the minefields of his young life. My loving wife should expect my best efforts as a husband, yet I sometimes feel selfish, distracted, and too worn out to give her the 100 percent she deserves. Yet all of my shortcomings are somehow overcome when I pray for the intercession of Saint Joseph and reflect on his heroic example in caring for Jesus and Mary.

Saint Augustine

As I continue to study the Catholic faith, I am drawn to the writings of Saint Augustine and his story of conversion. I feel a connection to this doctor of the Church because we have something in common: Both our mothers prayed for many years that we would come to know Jesus Christ. Saint Monica prayed for her son to give up his paganism and immoral lifestyle while my Baptist mother prayed that I would leave the spiritual wilderness and be reconciled to Christ. I am certain my Baptist mother did not have the Catholic Church in mind while she prayed, but nevertheless her prayers and those of Saint Monica were answered. I also feel drawn to this quote from Saint Augustine, which so accurately describes my own restless heart and search for the Truth: "You have created us for yourself, and our heart is restless until it rests in you."[22]

When I think about my faith journey and the road before me that still must be traveled, I know I can rely on the intercessions of these four great saints—and so many others—when I am in need. Their examples of faithfulness, joy, love, and endured suffering inspire and encourage me in so many ways. I am an unworthy sinner, but I know that I must strive every day to become a saint. A life focused on anything less would be a tragedy.

Part Three:

STRUGGLES
and LESSONS
LEARNED

CHAPTER 11

Noise

Upon Reflection

*"What I realized as I recalled the highly caffeinated
and frantic pace I had been keeping was that
I was acting like the workaholic I thought I had rid
myself of years ago when I converted to the Church."*

IN JANUARY 2007, I became a eucharistic guardian at my parish, which is blessed to have perpetual eucharistic adoration. This hour each week in the True Presence of Christ has been an incredible blessing in my life and the reflection and prayer time has been the inspiration for much of my writing. I distinctly remember going to eucharistic adoration one morning a few years ago with a sincere desire to be still and listen. I usually have too much "noise" in my life and I wanted to offer up my burdens in prayer to our Lord, ask for help, and patiently listen for his response. My mind remained calm and peaceful for only a short period of time before the usual cacophony of annoying voices in my head began to sound off with, "Why hasn't Jesus answered me yet?" "I wonder if my 9 a.m. meeting will go well." "I have a million e-mails to answer." And, "I wonder what's for dinner." I was in the chapel for five minutes and I was already in trouble!

Rather than give in to frustration, I decided to think about my actions and examine where I was falling short. I said a quick prayer and asked for guidance as I replayed the events of the previous months in my mind. What I realized as I recalled the highly caffeinated and frantic pace I had been keeping was that I was acting like the workaholic I thought I had rid myself of years ago when I converted to the Church. Instead of enjoying the quiet prayer and reflection I so dearly love early each morning at my home, I was filling that time with work on the *Integrated Catholic Life* eMagazine, answering e-mails, and doing research on my first book. The Jesuit Daily Examen that provided me brief moments of prayer and reflection throughout my busy day had been crowded out by meetings, calls, and other excuses. The laptop had been getting pulled out right after the kids went to bed rather than my usual 9:30 p.m. That eclipsed the time when my wife and I usually enjoyed some quiet moments together. I felt like I was racing toward a cliff and I needed a course correction.

Quiet prayer was not working, and reflecting on my recent hectic schedule left me feeling deflated. So I decided to focus on my spiritual reading to look for inspiration and help. I have found great comfort and wisdom over the years in the writings of Francis Fernandez and his wonderful series of books *In Conversation with God*. I turned to the meditation for that day in Volume 3, which is on the dignity of work. The light bulb went off for me a few minutes later as I read the passage I so desperately needed: "Work should not take up so much of our day that it occupies the time that should be dedicated to God, to the family, to our friends....If this should happen it would be a clear sign that we are not sanctifying ourselves through our work, but rather we are simply seeking self-satisfaction in it."[23] I had allowed myself to think that my hard work in my professional career and service to the Church was always for others, when perhaps one of my motivations had been for my own self-satisfaction. It was hard to admit, but I think there was some truth to it.

I circled back in my mind to how I had begun my hour of adoration when I asked our Lord for help. From the gift of self-awareness he gave me in reflecting on my recent behaviors to the realization that I need to make some changes and the epiphany he revealed to me in the writings of Francis Fernandez, Jesus absolutely answered my prayer that day. He gave me all that I asked for and everything he knew I needed. After that hour I knew I would have some hard work and a lot of prayer in front of me to make the necessary changes. I needed to restore peace and a sense of balance.

The problem of noise, distractions, and losing sight of what is truly important may be a common problem for many of us, and I fully recognize that I will be addressing this issue for the rest of my life. It is difficult in today's world to find peace, but I am committed to asking the Holy Spirit for help and guidance to reach this goal whenever I lose my way. The experience rattled me as my overactive brain would not allow me to be calm. I knew I needed to make some changes but was not quite sure where to begin.

The weeks following this experience were a combination of maintaining my typical fast pace, snatches of inconsistent prayer time and infrequent reflection on how I had gotten so far off course. Then I got sick. I had to cancel my meeting schedule for a whole week, as well as a few speaking events, and was forced to work from home as I regained my health. In retrospect, I now recognize the hand of God in this forced "retreat" and this was a warning to slow down a bit.

My crazy schedule had been forcibly addressed and a few valuable lessons had been learned about not ignoring my health, but I was still struggling with the noise issue as we were approaching Ash Wednesday. I had still not decided what I would give up for Lent when I joined my family for Mass that evening and was pondering the usual dilemma between giving up sugar or coffee. Then I heard a riveting homily from our parochial vicar, Father Henry Atem. He talked about removing the obstacles between us and Christ during Lent. He challenged us to examine what was getting in the way of a stronger relationship with him and to give up those things during Lent. The light bulb went off and I realized that I desperately needed more quiet time. I would never have peace and a return to the rich prayer life I once enjoyed unless I eliminated my distractions. So, I gave up radio, TV, and unnecessary computer time during that Lent, and have minimized these distractions as much as possible since then. The change has had an enormous impact on my life!

Before you decide that I'm nuts and this is not doable, indulge me for a little longer. I am in my car more than ninety minutes each day. By turning off the radio and enjoying the silence, I have turned formerly unproductive time into wonderful reflection and prayer time. Eliminating most TV has helped me reconnect to my spiritual reading in the evening. I have eliminated unnecessary computer time outside of my work and *Integrated Catholic Life* editing responsibilities, and I have carved out more meaningful time with my family. All of this is helping me more fully live up to the commitment I made in chapter three regarding my priorities in life. I must have been dense not to have done all of this sooner! The peace and stronger relationship with Christ I crave is getting nearer every day. And I am determined to get there with the help of the Holy Spirit.

What have I learned from these experiences? All of my hard work is meaningless if it is not given up for his greater glory instead of my personal satisfaction. I have learned that I am not Superman and I need to be careful about overscheduling my life. The commotion and hectic pace of the lives we lead aren't going away. But our reactions can improve our spirits and our relationships with our Lord. If we make regular, deliberate efforts to unplug from the chaos (however necessary and productive it might be) and reconnect with God in prayer and silence, that may perhaps be the best use of the scarce time we have. My pride often gets in the way, but during that Lenten season I was taught valuable lessons in humility. I was reminded of how comforting it is to seek the intercession and help of our Blessed Mother. Finally, I know I was made for heaven and not this place. I may always be stumbling toward peace and my final destination, but at least I am on the right path and moving forward. And that is a good place to start.

CHAPTER 12

Time

Where Does Faith Fit Into **My Busy Life?**

"Time is precious, and there are only so many minutes in the day, but I argue that we can more effectively integrate our faith, family, and work without sacrificing our livelihoods."

FOR YEARS I have heard people say they don't have enough time to pray, get involved in parish ministry, attend daily Mass, take part in eucharistic adoration, be involved in children's activities, serve in the community, etc. This complaint is so pervasive that, along with silos and surrender, I have identified our misconceptions about time as one of the biggest obstacles to leading an integrated Catholic life. As someone who is also challenged about having enough time each day, I wonder: Do we own our calendars or do our calendars own us?

Friends and colleagues have long wondered how I seem to squeeze so much activity into each day. As a reformed workaholic, I have always had a tendency to be fully engaged throughout the day and usually maintain a full plate of faith, family, and work-related activities. As I have gotten older and hopefully wiser, I have thought a great deal about how to make "time" work for me as I seek to grow as a Catholic, husband, father, business leader, and servant of the community. There is no magic bullet, but I would like to share five ideas for how we can begin to tame our calendars and lead fuller, richer, integrated lives:

- **Have our priorities in order.** Are we trying to juggle serving Christ, work, and family responsibilities each day? Is Christ sometimes an inconvenient add-on to an already packed schedule? Stop. Let's change our mindsets. As I shared in chapter three, we should be serving Christ first, family second, and work third on our list of life priorities. Being lights for Christ and serving him trumps everything! Second, our true vocation is to help our families, ourselves, and everyone else get to heaven. Third, our work should be given up for his greater glory and to serve the needs of our families. The "Big Three" should be followed by our health, friends, and other things important to us.

- **We control our calendars; our calendars do not control us.** The most common complaint I hear about time is: "My calendar is full and I can't squeeze that (prayer, Mass, service, etc.) in." Who enters the activity into our calendar? We do. With the new priority list in mind, let's start scheduling around Mass, prayer, family dinner, kids' activities, community service, exercise, etc. If you are in an environment with a rigid calendar controlled by others, think about what you can get accomplished before work, during lunch, and after work, and do the best you can. You may find more relevant help in the next few ideas.

- **Combine activities when possible.** This concept has worked well for me. When I go for a run or get on the treadmill, I pray the rosary. My wife and I use our time going to and from sports practices/activities to talk about life, faith, or whatever is on our minds. Keep a Bible or some other great faith-based book in your car or bag to read when you are waiting on an appointment. If you want to serve in the community, you can take your spouses and children along and do it as a family activity. There are a number of ways, but the combining concept is very easy to implement.

- **Remove the unnecessary and replace it with the necessary.** Want to pray more? Get up fifteen minutes earlier and pray the Morning Offering and the Angelus before leaving home. Add an Examen to your calendar and create five very short periods each day for reflection and prayer. Want to spend more quality time together as a family? Kill the TV and video games and replace them with talking, praying, reading, or outdoor activities. Go to reconciliation and eucharistic adoration together as a family. Want to start attending daily Mass more often? Start by giving up one early morning or lunch hour each week and attend Mass at our home parishes or one near where we work. Are the demands of work the cause of your issues (travel, demanding bosses, can't turn off e-mail, etc.)? We should ask ourselves whether we have become attached to a larger-than-needed lifestyle that our career is supporting and consider making a change. Downsizing your lifestyle may even be the ultimate answer.

- **Know where we are going.** All of these ideas should help us on our journey to heaven. We are made for our heavenly home and not this world. Our busy lives and daily activities should lead us to this end. Are our lives ordered to this purpose or do we serve other priorities that are of this world and not as important?

It is also vitally important to find quiet time for ourselves when we can detach, reflect, think, pray, exercise, and restore our energy before we jump back into the daily grind. The concept of leisure is an alien one to our culture, but we need to find that time to restore our mental, emotional, and spiritual energy. One idea, if you are married, is to work out an arrangement with your spouse each week to give each other the gift of guilt-free time to relax and detach. It is important, and I need to personally do a better job in this area.

Let's take control of our lives and not let the calendar become an excuse for avoiding what is important and necessary. I know in these difficult economic times it can be challenging to recalibrate our thinking about priorities, especially if we think it will affect how we earn a living. Time is precious, and there are only so many minutes in the day, but I argue that we can more effectively integrate our faith, family, and work without sacrificing our livelihoods. It comes down to recognizing the need, a sincere desire to change, and creative scheduling.

Do we really want to stand before Christ some day and say we could not fit in time to joyfully serve him during our lives on earth? I think we know the answer.

CHAPTER 13

At My Worst

Overcoming **My Worst Spiritual Behavior**

*"The lure of our fast-paced world and
our own spiritual lukewarmness can easily lead us
astray if we are not diligent and careful."*

I SOMETIMES marvel at my consistency. On a day—not long ago—filled with self-reflection, I realized that once again I was falling into repetitive bad behaviors that were hampering my faith journey. The last time I felt like this was just before Lent a few years ago; when I was overworked, worn out, and struggling to find peace. With the help of prayer, eucharistic adoration, reconciliation, and caring Catholic friends, I pulled back from the proverbial cliff at that time and returned to the right path. Although not as severe this time, I could feel myself edging closer to the cliff, and I needed to apply the brakes.

One of the supposed benefits of getting older is that we acquire wisdom gained from our lives. I am not sure I am any wiser, but I have tried to learn from my experiences. It occurred to me as I wrote this chapter that I needed to identify the challenges and bad behaviors that were causing me so many problems if I want to avoid coming back to this place in the future. Here is a partial list of behaviors that signal I may be on my "worst spiritual behavior":

- I have an iPhone addiction and struggle to put it down and stop checking e-mail.
- I work hard and get things done quickly, but I only wind up creating more space on the calendar that I fill with other projects.
- Leisure is not in my vocabulary when I am on my worst spiritual behavior.
- The work itself becomes more important than the goal, which should be to glorify Christ, provide for my family, and be a good steward in the community.
- I make excuses for missing daily Mass and the weeks pile up between visits to our priests for reconciliation.
- Instead of finding quiet moments to pray, I do it on the run and am usually going somewhere.
- Instead of being salt and light in the world, I get absorbed into the secular culture and don't reflect my Christ-inspired joy to anyone.
- My ministry work becomes burdensome and I feel weighed down instead of grateful for the opportunity to serve our Lord.
- I try to be in charge when I should be surrendering control to Christ.

Each of these bad behaviors adversely affects my faith, my relationship with my children, and my marriage. My health suffers. I become the "friend who is too busy" and am not as accessible to others as I should be. My attempts at spiritual reading are impeded by either too much work or fatigue, and I certainly don't feel like writing. Most importantly, my relationship with Christ suffers because I have foolishly placed countless barriers between us.

Enough is enough.

A friend told me early in my conversion that we all struggle in our spiritual lives, and it is a good thing to recognize that and keep pressing forward in trying to grow as a Catholic. I believe this is true and realize I have experienced growth over the years, often in spite of myself. Writing this openly about my struggles is certainly a sign of growth, I hope! I have a tendency to make things more complicated than they should be, and I need to focus on the theme of simplification if I want to break out of this recurring cycle. Here is my basic checklist to help me return to "spiritual wellness" when I get off track:

- Commit to an hour or more of prayer each day, with at least thirty minutes in a quiet place. The first prayer of every day will be a simple thank you to our Lord for the blessings I have received.

- Spend more electronic-free quality time with my family during which we read, walk, ride bikes, or play games together.

- Devote more time and attention to my wonderful wife. I will be "present" and not distracted when we are together.

- Go to at least one daily Mass a week.

- Spend at least thirty minutes a day reading my favorite Catholic authors or Scripture.

- Have coffee or lunch with a good friend once a week and seek feedback on how I am doing. Humbly accept fraternal correction if given.

- Walk/run or use my treadmill thirty minutes a day, five days a week, realizing there is a direct connection between my physical health and my spiritual health. Pray a rosary while exercising.

- Find quiet time for myself, especially on weekends, just to relax, think, read, or whatever....

- Find a silent retreat to attend each year.

- Go to reconciliation at least once a month.

- Seek the guidance and help of a spiritual director.

We are called to be in the world but not of the world and recognize that our ultimate goal is heaven. The lure of our fast-paced world and our own spiritual lukewarmness can easily lead us astray if we are not diligent and careful. I am certain that I will slip up many times on my journey, but Christ will always lead me back if I ask for his help. I am a busy guy with a lot on my plate, but all of that is meaningless if I am not pursuing a life of holiness and working hard to help me, my family, and everybody I know get to heaven. I am becoming more-self-aware about my worst spiritual behaviors, and with the help of the Holy Spirit I am working to overcome them. How about you?

CHAPTER 14

Being a Man of God

Lessons for a Catholic Man

*"Over the years since my conversion into the Church,
I have become increasingly self-aware about
my shortcomings and how they negatively impact
the practice of my faith."*

I HAD AN EPIPHANY as I was preparing myself for reconciliation not long ago and realized that I was about to confess many of the same sins I have been struggling with for years. It dawned on me that particular morning that I had made progress in some areas, but felt that I was going backward in others. Didn't Einstein once say that the definition of insanity is "doing the same thing over and over again and expecting different results?"

I spoke with a few Catholic brothers the next day and they readily confirmed facing the same problem: We all struggle to break out of repetitive sinful behaviors and avoid self-created obstacles to drawing closer to Christ. We also agreed that we desire a closer relationship with him, we all want to get to heaven with our families and we all want to be devout in the practice of our Catholic faith. So where do we slip up? Why do we fall short?

I hope to offer some useful insight to help other Catholic men and the women in their lives be more aware of these self-created challenges and take the necessary steps to overcome them. I will start by listing a few general observations about men that may be uncomfortable to read and acknowledge:

- We often struggle with humility and let our pride and egos get in the way.

- We like to be in control.

- We can be stubborn and inflexible to change.

- Our identities are often wrapped up in our careers.

- We struggle to ask others (especially the Lord) for help.

- We are often inclined to action when reflection and discernment are more appropriate.

- We are often uncomfortable with open displays of emotion (ours and others').

- We may be overly concerned about the opinions of others (that is: What will our buddies think?).

(Women, feel free to think of a list for you). Do these observations resonate with you? This last may sound harsh, but my intention is to illustrate some of the obstacles between us and Christ. OK, we have acknowledged the problem...now what? Let's explore how to get on the right path and stay there.

Over the years since my conversion into the Church, I have become increasingly self-aware about my shortcomings and how they negatively impact the practice of my faith. Knowing the challenge is only half of the equation. I must be willing to address them (remember—guys are inclined toward action!). Before we begin, let's examine what we know for certain: We have a goal (heaven), a road map (Scripture and tradition), examples to follow (the saints), leadership (the pope, bishops, priests, and deacons), clear teaching authority (the magisterium of the Church), help along the way (the sacraments), and divine guidance (the Holy Spirit). It is obvious that we have the tools and resources we need.

Let's consider how we can make progress and stay on the right path. I don't know about you, but if I can't form the solution to a problem into an actionable and achievable goal, I will often struggle. Here is a list of eight practical actions I am working on. I hope you find them helpful:

1. **Surrender.** We have to surrender to Christ on an ongoing basis for his will to be done in our lives. Guys, we are not in charge...as much as we want to be! "Whoever finds his life will lose it, and whoever loses his life for my sake will find it" (Matthew 10:39).

2. **Pray.** Work on developing a daily prayer routine with the goal of at least an hour a day devoted to prayer. Sound difficult? Think about how much TV we watch a day. Consider how much time we spend in our cars each day and how much time we devote to exercise. We have more than enough time for prayer if we plan for it, schedule it and commit to it. Pray the Morning Offering or other prayer before you leave home = ten minutes. Pray the rosary in your car or while exercising = twenty minutes. The Daily Jesuit Examen = fifteen minutes. Prayer with all meals = five minutes. Prayer with our children and spouse = ten minutes. Add it up: We just did an hour of prayer.

3. **Become passionate about the Eucharist.** Want to fully experience Christ and be closer to him? Seek out the True Presence of Christ in the Eucharist in daily Mass when possible and spend quiet time before the blessed sacrament in eucharistic adoration every week. My time in adoration is definitely the most impactful and helpful hour of my week.

4. **Go to reconciliation more frequently.** As I wrote in chapter five, we are hopefully praying and asking for God's help with our burdens, but we are still saddled with the sins we commit daily. Go to a priest and partake of this wonderful gift we Catholics enjoy but may not use enough: the sacrament of reconciliation. Commit to going once a month. A thorough examination of conscience and honest confession will lift our spirits and keep us on the right path!

5. **Accept and study our faith.** Accepting the teaching of our Church is necessary, but so is the knowledge that our full understanding may take time. Trust that two millennia of Church teaching is probably much more reliable than what you or I might conjure up on our own. Go to a parish Bible study, take apologetics classes, read Scripture and the catechism, and read great Catholic authors who are faithful to the magisterium.

6. **Practice detachment.** Let's ask ourselves whether we really need "it," whatever "it" is. Let go of the material things that are in the way of our prayer lives, church attendance, charitable giving, friendships, volunteering, and certainly our relationships with Christ. The catechism says, "Detachment from riches is necessary for entering the Kingdom of heaven."[24]

7. **Understand our true vocation.** For those of us blessed to be married and have children, we must recognize that helping our families get to heaven and being good husbands and fathers encompass our real vocation (not our business careers). It is so easy to allow our families to serve our work (my issue many years ago) instead of having our work serve our families...and in turn, our families to serve the Lord.

8. **Be courageous.** Christians are meant to stand out, not blend in. Blending in speaks to conforming and making sacrifices so our faith becomes part of the mainstream...and we need to fight it! We live in difficult, trying times. Families are under attack, our

children are at risk, many people are blind to the need to respect and value all life, and atheists are one of the fastest-growing groups in the world. We have an opportunity to be beacons of light and good examples of Christ's redeeming love. We will be judged one day on the fruits of our apostolate, and we hope to hear Jesus say the words, "Well done, good and faithful servant."

This list may look like a lot of hard work, but the real challenge is to practice these actions not as a bunch of new "to-dos," but as part of a broader, unifying approach to a balanced and meaningful life that places Christ first in all areas of our lives. I simply want to encourage all of us to remember that we are called to lead lives of holiness, and we are made for heaven. As Catholic men, we have a responsibility to be strong fathers and husbands, leaders in our parishes, good stewards in the community, and humble followers of our Lord. Look to the example of Saint Joseph, patron saint of fathers and the universal Church for his obedience, humility, selflessness, courage, and the love he showed to Mary and Jesus. If we can emulate Saint Joseph even a little each day, we will be that much closer to becoming the men we are called to be.

CHAPTER 15

Parenting

The Challenges of **Modern Parenthood**

*"I asked God for help and a path to follow
that would help me step up to my responsibilities and
for the peace and courage to deal with being
a father in these challenging times."*

SOMETIMES I can almost imagine myself as a great father to my children...then I do something to mess it up. I vividly recall a past October when the boys and I welcomed my wife home from a five-day trip to California where she had been visiting her sister. What started out as my great adventure with the kids at the beginning of her trip turned into exhaustion at the end, and I guiltily looked forward to my wife's coming home so I could escape to my work and other activities. I had just experienced a great time with my sons (we really did have fun), and now I was looking to flee the scene and go back to activities that aren't nearly as important. What was my problem?

This isn't a self-reflective pity party but a candid acknowledgment of the ongoing challenges I face to provide my sons with the father/ role model I believe they deserve. I want them to grow up to be good men and great fathers, and I feel like every moment I am with them is a learning opportunity. I want to teach them about our beautiful Catholic faith, what the real world is like, the difference between right and wrong, the importance of values, etc. The list of lessons they need to learn is endless, yet I hate to admit that because of the enormous demands on my time during the day I sometimes look forward to their bedtime so my wife and I can get a break. I know we need time as a couple and I need my free time as well, but I still feel guilty.

I carried these thoughts into the weekend and did a lot of praying. I asked God for help and a path to follow that would help me step up to my responsibilities, and for the peace and courage to deal with being a father in these challenging times. Maybe I needed to see role models and examples to help me get closer to the better father I want to be.

Well, sometimes God answers prayer very promptly and clearly.

After that weekend of prayer and reflection, I had four powerful reminders of the real meaning of fatherhood in the days that followed. The hand of God was clearly at work in forcing me to slow down long enough to recognize and absorb these lessons:

On that Tuesday afternoon I was driving back from a doctor visit with my oldest son when I decided to call my father in Florida. We exchanged idle chitchat for a few minutes, then I shared my recent fatherhood dilemma with him. He listened silently. When I finished, he offered this sage observation: "Randy, I think you need to give yourself a break. I was never a perfect father and I made my share of mistakes, but I always knew God would find a way to help me and make up for my shortcomings. I also think one of the best things I did for you and your sister was to make sure you knew how much I loved your mom."

I reflected on the conversation with my father as we walked into Mass for All Saints Day: not perfect...God will help me...love my wife. I began thinking of Saint Joseph and his amazing example as a husband and a father. He was a good and simple man who trusted God, took a pregnant Mary as his wife and raised Jesus as his own son as the head of the Holy Family. As I shared in chapter 10, I have always found peace by asking Saint Joseph for his intercession, and

I did so again on All Saints Day. In my own father and in the patron saint of fathers I had rediscovered my role models.

The next day was a bit traumatic for my family, as my oldest son was to have a tube placed in his left ear for the eighth time. As you read in the first chapter, he has high-functioning autism. He was very anxious about the operation as we drove to the outpatient surgery center. All went well, and I was relieved to see him as they rolled his bed into the room where I was waiting. I looked down on my firstborn and stroked his hair, finding it hard to believe he was a teenager. The outpouring of love I felt at that moment for my son and his younger brother reminded me of the joys of being a father and of what is important in life. God created these children and gave them to my wife and me. We are truly blessed to be their parents.

After getting my son home for my wife to take care of him, I returned to a pile of work at the office and plowed through it as fast as possible so I could get home and see how he was doing. As I walked in the door feeling tired, distracted, and a little guilty (again), my younger son ran up to me with a poster he had made in school. He said, "Dad, what do you think of my poster? Take a look at the bottom on the left. Do you like it?" The section was called "My Hero," and he described his hero this way:

> *He spends a lot of time with me and tells me things.*
> *He plays sports with me and takes me to lacrosse practice.*
> *We pray together.*
> *He started writing books not long ago and*
>   *I am very proud of him.*
> *I want to write like him some day.*
> *My hero is my dad.*

After wiping a few tears away it dawned on me that if we ever want to get a report card on how we are doing, maybe we should ask our children.

Have you or someone you love been through the same kinds of struggles I have experienced? They have taught me that I can't carry the burden of being a father by myself. I need to be humble and ask for help. I will more frequently seek out the sage advice of my father, the intercession of Saint Joseph, and most importantly seek the help of our heavenly Father in prayer. I will make sure my kids know how much I love their mother. If I do these things faithfully, I will more fully experience the blessings and joys of being a father to these wonderful boys.

Part Four

AUTHENTICITY, COURAGE, *and the* INTEGRATED CATHOLIC LIFE

CHAPTER 16

Boredom

Rethinking Catholic Boredom

"Boredom is a side effect of our fast-paced, materialistic culture. We feel bored because we are constantly being overstimulated and sold on the idea that we can have it all now and that something better is always around the corner."

ONE SATURDAY MORNING my youngest son said: "Dad, I'm bored. What are we going to do for fun today?" Knowing him well, I translated this to mean that he was looking for something new and exciting, and I was supposed to provide it. This all too frequent discussion with my children has been the cause of considerable reflection of late. As adults, do we also seek frequent engagement and entertainment? Does this desire for fun and excitement ever spill over into how we view our Catholic faith?

I often hear complaints that "Mass is boring," "The priest is difficult to understand" or "The priest didn't wow us with an exciting homily." Still more complaints (whining?) center on the lack of exciting music during Mass, the "inconvenience" of having to attend Mass weekly as well as all the holy days of obligation. I also frequently hear this comment: "I wish our parish was more like >>insert name of any Protestant church<< Church. They have a lot of fun in their services and the music is awesome." The list of complaints is likely much longer, but I think you get the picture.

Are We Suffering From Spiritual A.D.D.?

Much has been written about the explosion of Attention Deficit Disorder (A.D.D.) diagnoses in the past few decades. Many studies link kids' overstimulation from video games as a big contributor to the problem. Adults have the same challenges as we struggle with our own addictions to smart phones and information overload from computers, TV, etc. Is this problem extending into our spiritual lives? Do we go from parish to parish looking for some sort of "Catholic buzz" to keep us entertained? Do we flirt with heresy by attending non-Catholic churches? Are our brains, craving more and more stimulation, incapable of finding peace? We need to tune out the "noise" to achieve the quiet and focus required in the Mass. This has been an ongoing issue for me and countless others I know.

Spiritual Shepherd or Entertainer-in-Chief?

Do we ever take a moment to consider the challenging life of a Catholic priest? In addition to being our spiritual shepherds, parish priests are the administrators of complex organizations often beset with unique problems ranging from people issues to budget shortfalls. Their days are filled with celebrating Mass; presiding at weddings, funerals and baptisms; hearing confessions; visiting the sick; prayer; study; meetings with parishioners, and dozens of other duties we may not fully appreciate. They are *not* our entertainment directors. Before we complain about something these men of God do or don't do, we should reflect a little and say a prayer of thanksgiving for their lifelong commitment to help us attain heaven. These good men need our prayers and our support every single day. They do *not* need nor deserve much of the criticism that is sent their way.

The Eucharist

Do you ever notice that entering church for Mass these days often resembles people finding their seats in a theater before a movie begins?

There is lots of noise and chitchat all the way up to the beginning of Mass. Where is the reverence? The respect? The humility? Time spent preparing to enter into the mysteries? We are about to receive holy Communion, the body and blood, soul and divinity of our Lord Jesus Christ, but we sometimes treat this sacred time like a secular family reunion instead of a holy celebration. Maybe one of the reasons people feel bored with the Mass is they have forgotten that the center of the Mass is Jesus Christ in the eucharistic sacrifice. "The Christian faithful are to hold the Most Holy Eucharist in highest honor, taking an active part in the celebration of the most august sacrifice, receiving this sacrament most devoutly and frequently, and worshiping it with the highest adoration. In explaining the doctrine about this sacrament, pastors of souls are to teach the faithful diligently about this obligation."[25]

A Little Self-Awareness and a Desire to Change

If anything you have read so far sounds familiar and hits too close to home, there may be a problem and change is needed. Too often we don't know how our behavior is coming across to others until we hear it from a friend. More importantly, if we are in the "complainer camp," can we change course? A thorough and honest examination of conscience provides an excellent way to identify our sinful behavior before having those sins forgiven by a priest in the sacrament of reconciliation. With more self-awareness and a contrite heart, it is only logical that we can now focus on what is really important about the Mass and better understand the critical role the Church plays in our lives.

We Can't Be Bored if We Are Sincerely Seeking Him

Boredom is a side effect of our fast-paced, materialistic culture. We feel bored because we are constantly being overstimulated and sold on the idea that we can have it all now and that something better is always around the corner. As rational human beings, we must realize that this is neither true nor sustainable. If we are sincerely seeking Christ, we will find him through the Church he founded.

The world offers **celebrities** to idolize...the Church offers **saints** to follow.

The world offers **noise**...the Church offers **peace**.

The world offers **false dreams**...the Church offers the **Truth**.

The world offers and celebrates **vice**...the Church offers a life of **virtue**.

The world offers **earthly pleasures**...the Church offers **eternal heaven**.

A Cure for Catholic Boredom in Six Easy Steps

Every issue I have written about in this chapter has been an ongoing challenge for me and countless other people I know. We must realize this is not healthy behavior. How do we change? To sum up, here are ways to overcome the key points you have read, summarized into "Six Steps to Cure Catholic Boredom":

1. **We have to turn off at least some of the noise.** Our spiritual A.D.D. is fed by our addiction to an overdose of input from various sources. As I shared in chapter eleven, try to not listen to the radio in the car. Eliminate most, if not all, TV time. Read more books. Get outside more often. Find time for quiet reflection and prayer every day.

2. **Show more respect for our priests and quit looking to them for entertainment.** They are not here to make Mass "exciting." We are at Mass to offer worship and receive the Eucharist, not to hear a blockbuster homily or loud music.

3. **Have we prayed to be worthy to receive Jesus?** Have we thanked God for this gift? Have we prayed to let others see Christ in us? Reverence...gratitude...humility...worship....These are the key words to remember about the Mass.

4. **Go to reconciliation as often as possible.** Do a thorough and honest examination of conscience. Where have we fallen short? Confess these sins to a priest and be forgiven. We will be less critical and eliminate boredom if we are acutely aware of our thinking and behaviors that lead to these avoidable sins.

5. **Get involved and make a difference.** Sitting on the outside and complaining is boring. Why not join a parish ministry and contribute our time and talent in a more productive way?

6. **Quit trying to please both the world and God.** "No one can serve two masters. He will either hate one and love the other, or be devoted to one and despise the other. You cannot serve God and mammon" (Matthew 6:24).

Feeling bored about our Catholic faith is subtle and dangerous—it sort of creeps up on you. When we are bored we tend to be critical and seek more excitement. This is the wrong path. The world offers us false gods and tries to paint a negative picture of Catholicism that is an illusion. We have to fight through these lies. Perceived boredom may lead some to leave the Church for other faiths. They are drawn to the excitement and buzz, but will learn in time that they had everything they needed in the Church Jesus founded. Let's reflect on how we feel right now about the Mass, priests, church, etc. If we feel bored or critical, let's follow a sound road map to bring us back from this dangerous territory. We have so much to be thankful for as Catholics if we will only take the time to appreciate it. The choice is ours, and I humbly pray that we will make the right one.

CHAPTER 17

Human Respect

What Others **Think of Us**

*"I wonder we if ever stop and reflect on how often
our public actions and thinking are overly influenced
by what others may think about our Catholic faith."*

I HAVE HAD numerous conversations with friends and professional
acquaintances over the years on the subject of openly sharing our
Catholic faith. I am always a little surprised at how often many of
them express strong reluctance to being open about their beliefs. The
reasons given have included, "I don't want to offend anyone," "We
could never do that at work," and "I don't like to discuss that outside
of my parish." I wonder we if ever stop and reflect on how often our
public actions and thinking are overly influenced by what others may
think about our Catholic faith. This comes up so often that I have
dedicated a chapter to the issue.

I wonder how many times a day we miss opportunities to stand
up for Christ or share our faith. Is it the conversation we avoid with
a troubled coworker? Is it standing up to someone who is attacking
the Church? How about the person who is quietly curious about the
Catholic faith and is only waiting on an invitation to attend Mass with
us? Too often a misplaced concern for the opinions of those around us
keeps us from embracing our responsibilities as Catholics. However,
it is crystal clear that Jesus expects us to openly share our faith and be

overt witnesses for him, if we read the Gospel of Matthew 10:32–33, "Everyone who acknowledges me before others I will acknowledge before my heavenly Father. But whoever denies me before others, I will deny before my heavenly Father."

Christ always taught the Truth regardless of the audience and is our greatest example on how to not be concerned about the respect of others. His enemies recognized this aspect of Christ's teaching in Matthew 22:16: "'Teacher, we know that you are a truthful man and that you teach the way of God in accordance with the truth. And you are not concerned with anyone's opinion, for you do not regard a person's status.'"

Francis Fernandez, author of *In Conversation with God*, makes this relevant observation (about sharing the truth regardless of the repercussions): "Christ asks his disciples to imitate him in this practice. Christians should foster and defend their well-earned professional, moral and social prestige, since it belongs to the essence of human dignity. This prestige is also an important component of our personal apostolate. Yet we should not forget that our conduct will meet with opposition from those who openly oppose Christian morality and those who practice a watered-down version of the faith. It is possible that the Lord will ask of us the sacrifice of our good name, and even of life itself. With the help of his grace we will struggle to do his will. Everything we have belongs to the Lord."[26]

I feel sorely challenged by the words in the preceding paragraph, yet I know we are all called to have courage and make sacrifices in his name. If we have faith and trust in Christ we will receive the grace we need. I also realize that our behavior will be a clear example to others of the strength of our faith. Many non-believers or lukewarm Christians may be moved to a deeper faith if they witness our good and sincere example.

Whether you are a business person, in career transition, a stay-at-home parent, a student or a senior citizen, chances are you have faced this struggle with worrying about what others think of us. It is a natural human tendency that affects me and everyone I know. We all want to be liked, respected, and included. But here's the catch: We can't separate our spiritual selves from our physical being. The faith we profess is part of who we are and can't be hidden away. "This split between the faith which many profess and their daily lives deserves to be counted among the more serious errors of our age. The Christian who neglects his temporal duties, neglects his duties toward his neighbor and even God, and jeopardizes his eternal salvation."[27]

Can we all agree that being "stealth Catholics" is not the answer? If so, here are five thoughts on how to overcome our fear of what others may think of us when publicly sharing our faith:

1. **Is there really a policy?** I have heard many times that expressing our faith in the workplace is "against company policy." Have we actually seen written policies that address making the sign of the cross and praying at meals, praying quietly at your desk, going to Mass at lunch or wearing ashes on our foreheads on Ash Wednesday? I know there may be exceptions, but let me challenge all of us to consider the possibility that much of our fear may be based on false perceptions of possible persecution and not reality.

2. **"Preach the Gospel at all times, use words if necessary."**[28] Please reflect on these words of wisdom attributed to Saint Francis of Assisi. It rarely occurs to us to think about our own faith journeys, the example we set for others and the Christ-inspired joy we should radiate as the most effective ways to share our faith. Letting others see Jesus Christ at work in us is a powerful form of witness that will attract others who want what we have in our lives.

3. **We should share first.** Why not be the one who breaks the ice by making reference to your family, challenges you are facing, vacation plans, a book you recently read, etc.? Start by sharing the easy things, encourage reciprocation by asking questions, then it's easy to look for opportunities to share our faith. Pray that the Holy

Spirit will provide opportunities for this sharing. If eating a meal with others, I have always found that saying a blessing and making the sign of the cross is an excellent catalyst for a conversation regarding faith. I have observed countless "guarded" conversations over the years in which individuals played it safe and politically correct. Let's move beyond banal and safe dialogue and instead be courageous and transparent. If we truly love Christ and his Church, we need to let that love-inspired joy be known to all!

4. **Pursuing heaven versus being popular.** Heaven is our ultimate destination. Will our critics help us get there? Will they stand up for us during tough times? No, they will pull us into a secular way of life that has little room for God and where materialism and popularity are the fashionable idols of the day. Francis Fernandez wrote that overcoming human respect is part of the virtue of fortitude. He describes the challenges a Christian may endure as "...rumors and calumnies, mockery, discrimination at work, the loss of economic opportunities, or superficial friendships. In these uncomfortable circumstances it may be tempting to take the easy way out and 'give in.' By such means we could avoid rejection, misunderstanding and ridicule. We could become concerned at the thought of losing friends, of 'closing doors' which we will later be unable to reopen. This is the temptation to be influenced by human respect, hiding one's true identity and forsaking our commitment to live as disciples of Christ."[29]

5. **Consistently pursue an integrated Catholic life.** Do we take our faith with us to work, meals with friends, the kids' soccer games, and neighborhood swim meets? Or do we only practice our Catholic faith at Mass on Sundays? It is easy to conform to secular expectations, but difficult to publicly show our love of Jesus, live out the Beatitudes, evangelize, and lead a fully integrated life. I have always found inspiration on this topic in the wisdom of Blessed John Paul II's apostolic exhortation *Christifideles Laici*:

"The unity of life of the lay faithful is of the greatest importance: indeed they must be sanctified in everyday professional and social life. Therefore, to respond to their vocation, the lay faithful must see their daily activities as an occasion to join themselves to God, fulfill his will, serve other people and lead them to communion with God in Christ."[30]

We must pray for the guidance of the Holy Spirit, as we can't do this alone. In my own experience, this is a daily work-in-progress, and it is never easy. We should recognize that there are others looking at our example who want to learn from us and be inspired by our courage, if we are only willing to take a stand for Christ. Think about how fortunate we are to live in a Christian country, despite the fact that our religious liberties are under attack. Fighting back and standing our ground in defense of our faith and religious freedom are part of our duty and our calling. In the early Church, to be openly Christian was to risk a martyr's death. It is sobering to realize that Christians are being persecuted in Pakistan, India, the Middle East, parts of Western Europe, and other parts of the world even as you read this chapter.

As difficult as it may sound, a sacrifice on our part is required. The sacrifice is simply to love Christ more than the good opinions of those around us. We should realize how little is being asked of us compared to what Jesus endured for us on the cross. As I stated earlier, the desire to be liked, respected, and popular is normal. I sometimes struggle with this, as do many of you. But let's pray for one another and continue to ask Jesus for courage, strength, and the discernment to know and follow his will and not be concerned about the opinions of others.

CHAPTER 18

Courage

The Consequences of the
"I Don't Want to Offend" Mindset

"There is a secular tidal wave sweeping across our country and much of the world. In the name of fairness, equality, and political correctness, we are asked (and sometimes forced) to accept things that are absolutely contrary to our faith."

IN CONTINUING the discussion from the last chapter, I recall a lunch last year with a longtime client. The blessing I said at the beginning of our meal was the catalyst for an interesting conversation (as it has been with so many others in the past). This human resources executive smiled as I made the sign of the cross at the end and said, "Well, I don't see this every day. I can't remember the last time I said a blessing over a meal at a business lunch." Once again, the simple act of saying a blessing over a meal in public was prompting a conversation about faith in the public square, as it has many times before, and I must admit that I eagerly jumped right in!

"Why do you think people, especially people of faith, avoid saying a blessing over their meals in public?" I asked. "I value your opinion as an HR professional and I also know from past conversations that you are a Christian. What do you think keeps people from expressing their faith in front of others?" She looked at me for a few minutes and said in a subdued voice, "I guess they don't want to offend other people."

I suspected this would be the answer, as I have observed countless people over the years who are extremely reluctant to be open about their faith. I have frequently written on this subject, but I want to narrowly focus in on this misguided idea that we are offending people by being open in the practice of our Catholic faith, beliefs, and values.

There is a secular tidal wave sweeping across our country and much of the world. In the name of fairness, equality, and political correctness, we are asked (and sometimes forced) to accept things that are absolutely contrary to our faith. Because we often "don't want to offend others" by speaking out or acting on our convictions, we are living with the following consequences:

- Political correctness is pervasive in business environments today, and we have too few leaders willing to stand up for their convictions and do the right things regardless of the consequences.

- "Merry Christmas" often gets watered down to the generic "Happy Holidays."

- Because many of us may be shying away from living out our faith in the public square, we run the risk of being "two-thirds Catholics" where we only live out our faith at home and at Mass on Sunday and ignore the one-third of our adult lives that we likely spend in the workplace. This split personality is toxic, as we can't possibly separate our spiritual beings from our physical selves.

- Religious liberties are under siege. The attacks on conscience protection clauses, the government forcing Catholic organizations to offer employees access to contraception and abortion through the HHS Mandate, the attack on the Defense of Marriage Act... the list is endless.

- Our silence in public may lead people to assume an implied acceptance on our part of things contrary to the teachings of our Church. Over time, this silence may even lead some of us down the path of defending and promoting the wrong positions on abortion, gay marriage, and other issues where Church teaching is crystal clear.

I suggest to you that the reasons people gravitate to the "I don't want to offend" position include fear of job loss, fear of being criticized or judged, fear of losing social status, poor understanding of the teachings of our Church or the belief that somebody else will stand up because we are too busy to get involved. The challenges I have identified are a sliver of the many we face because we don't want to offend anyone and are a direct result of our not acting on our beliefs. If even a modest percentage of the sixty-plus million Catholics in the U.S. openly embraced and acted on the principles of our faith, we would transform the entire world. Maybe the answer for many of us is to take small steps at first. A good place to start is wishing everyone a Blessed Advent and Merry Christmas. Pray over every meal and make the sign of the cross. Go to the voting booth and vote for pro-life candidates who support the teachings of the Church. Let's reflect on our actions each day and ask ourselves whether we can offer each of those actions up to God (the Jesuit Daily Examen is a helpful tool). Not everyone is called to heroic acts, so let's start where we can with what we have and grow from there.

The saddest and most glaring point about the "I don't want to offend" mindset is that we rarely think about how we are offending Christ. We get bogged down in minor personal concerns and our own fears when we should be thinking about his sacrifice for us on the cross. We should routinely fall to our knees in gratitude and recognize that nothing we will ever face can compare to what he did for us. We will be supported through our fears, difficulties and struggles if we will go to him in prayer and ask for help. His sacrifice *then* and his ongoing love and support *now* will always sustain us in difficult situations if we will only be humble, serve him, and love him.

We are called to lead lives of holiness. We have the Church Christ founded to guide us. We can be courageous because he is always with us. If others are truly offended at the mention of Christ's name or actions we take in his name, we should pray for them but not stop living out our faith.

We can make a difference if we are unafraid to be authentic Catholics and care less about offending others and more about giving offense to Jesus. The choices we make and the consequences of our actions are in our control. One courageous Catholic can set a great example. A group of courageous Catholics can change the world.

CHAPTER 19
Catholic Authenticity

Let's Get Real

*"I want to believe that deep down
most of us desire to consistently be our real selves
but don't know how to get there."*

WHY IS IT DIFFICULT to be the same person at work, home, church, and with our friends? I have observed this problem for most of my adult life, but lately I have become more aware of the challenges people have with consistently being "real." In discussions with friends, I often receive blank stares and perceive a lot of discomfort when I advocate for being the same person at all times and for being transparent about our lives with others. Why is authenticity, especially Catholic authenticity, so uncomfortable?

My instincts and own experience lead me to think the root cause of this occurred for many of us at a young age. The first time we felt pressure to "fit in" with a particular group in school, we began down the path of conformity that only accelerates as we grow older. In college, we may have heard from our professors (or our parents) that we need to keep work, faith, and our personal lives separate. Looking back, I believe one of the reasons for my agnosticism in college was the various the groups I associated with, and I wanted to fit in. I felt like two people as I acted the role of "partying agnostic" in public, but harbored secret doubts as I constantly went against what I had been taught by my parents. This was one of the most challenging times of my life, and I frequently reflect on this period as I think about my own sons and their futures.

After school, many of us may have feared being judged or criticized in those early jobs for sharing anything personal, and that only hardens into a compartmentalized mindset as we grow in our careers. This can manifest itself in a few different ways. In the early years of my career I observed a number of my peers and former classmates focusing on their careers and keeping their personal lives very separate. I can't really recall anything personal about the people I worked with; they never talked about themselves. As for myself, I had buried by former faith life so deeply that all I had in my life was work. I rarely dated, saw my friends infrequently, and worked as hard as possible to advance in my profession. As I shared in chapter one, I met and married my wife in my late twenties, and for the first time since my early teen years I felt truly happy. But I kept work and my family completely separate and was as far away from an integrated life as you could imagine. It was not until my personal surrender and conversion in 2005 that the walls I had built around the silos of my life came down. After that life-changing period, I have been able to more consistently lead a fully integrated life. The glue that holds it all together is my love for Christ and the practice of my Catholic faith.

What is your story? As you reflect on your life, does what I have written here resonate with you? I want to believe that deep down most of us desire to consistently be our real selves but don't know how to get there. Logic should tell us that it is harmful to suppress our true selves for a sustained period of time, yet many people perceive there is no other option. Do you love being a parent but feel awkward about discussing your kids at work? Do you desire to spend more time with your family but worry about speaking about this with your boss? Is your Catholic faith important to you, but do you avoid discussing it because of perceived intolerance among friends and work colleagues? Have you ever been faced with a difficult ethical or moral dilemma, but remained silent or chose the easy way out rather than advocate for doing the right thing? In my professional and personal circles I have encountered countless people who are struggling with these dilemmas. Despite my passion for the integrated and authentic Catholic life, this is still a challenge for me, and I find myself praying for help and guidance almost daily.

Obstacles to Authenticity

Let's address some of the obstacles that may prevent us from being authentic Catholics. I am making a base assumption that you agree with me on some level that authenticity is important and that many (though not all) people have a desire to be more open, transparent and authentic. Here are a few of the obstacles that prevent this from happening:

- There could be a lack of self-awareness. Do we even know that there is a problem? Fear of people not liking the real us. Fear of not fitting in. Fear of being judged. Fear of persecution for our religious beliefs. Fear of not moving up the career ladder if we don't fit the right corporate mold.

- Lack of confidence in our opinions. Lack of faith in our convictions. Lack of courage to defend the truth. Lack of knowledge about our faith.

- Attachment to an income level and lifestyle that requires unhealthy compromises.

- Conforming to society's march toward political correctness, universal tolerance and acceptance of things that are in direct conflict with our faith, values and principles.

- Relaxing our standards because it easier to go along with the crowd than take a stand.

This list may be as painful for you to acknowledge as it is for me...or you may have a different list. The questions I ask and the obstacles I talk about are unsettling but necessary if a more authentic life is to be pursued and embraced. It is a sad indictment of the times in which we live when it takes an act of courage for us to be our true selves.

Embracing the REAL You

Have you ever replayed pivotal moments in your life over in your head and regretted your actions or words? Ever feel a twinge when your mouth said one thing and your heart/head felt another? Perhaps these feelings are your conscience trying to get your attention. It could be the Holy Spirit. Maybe, just maybe, it is time to consistently let our true selves be seen by others. But is there an upside to having the courage to embrace who we really are?

The answer is a simple yes, because as I have shared repeatedly in this book, we are made for heaven and not this place. We are here to help ourselves, our families, and everyone else get to heaven.

I wrote this chapter from the perspective of my Catholic faith, although I believe anyone can find value in what I am saying. As a Catholic reaching out to other Catholics, I challenge all of us (including myself) to be brave and step up in our defense of Christ and his Church. The Church is under siege on multiple fronts and is often attacked for its unflinching defense of Christ's teachings. We can no longer remain passive and be Catholic only at Mass on Sundays but somebody different the rest of the week. Let's not allow ourselves to fall into an apathetic cultural Catholicism, but instead be authentically active in the practice of our faith. One person can absolutely make a positive difference in the world if we are courageous and willing to stand up for the truth of our faith. We can and should make a real difference through our prayers, our voices, our writing, and at the ballot box.

After you read this chapter, prayerfully consider whether you need to be more authentically Catholic. I don't know many of us who couldn't stand some improvement! Let's ask the Holy Spirit to guide our actions and give us courage. Let's be joyful and set a good example for others by being unafraid to be our true selves. What is required of us is not easy, but our Lord will help us if we offer up our burdens and concerns to him in prayer. He gave his life for us on the cross. This sacrifice requires a faithful, authentic, and courageous response from his followers.

With confidence and purpose, with our ultimate destination in mind, let's all try to be a little more authentic today.

CHAPTER 20

Joy

O Joyful Catholics, **Where Are You?**

*"For Catholics, joy in the midst of extreme adversity
is our obligation and our duty."*

I BELIEVE one of the greatest obstacles to evangelization and sharing our faith with others today is that many of us have forgotten how to be joyful. I know when the stresses of the world weigh me down, I struggle to maintain a joyful attitude in the presence of others. We are often so busy with our hectic schedules and materialistic lifestyles that we lose touch with our love of Christ and neglect our faith. What would consistently reflecting sincere joy do for our growth as Catholics? The people around us? For the rest of the world?

Think about it. The early Christians had the good fortune to be the first to share the Good News. Imagine the joy they felt in sharing Christ's message of love to everyone. They stood out as happy in a suffering world, just as Christians have an opportunity to do so today. Jesus promised the Apostles (and us) this joy at the Last Supper when he said in John 16:22: "So you also are now in anguish. But I will see you again, and your hearts will rejoice, and no one will take your joy away from you."

Do we show our joy at home, at work, with friends? We have so much to be truly thankful for in our relationship with Christ and the truth and beauty of our Catholic faith. But, being truly joyful should lead to sharing that joy and the ability to express the truths of our faith in a way that shows the depth of our sincere belief and love to others. "May the God of hope fill you with all joy and peace in believing, so that you may abound in hope by the power of the Holy Spirit" (Romans 15:13).

Saint Paul reinforces the call to be joyful in 1 Thessalonians 5:16–18: "Rejoice always. Pray without ceasing. In all circumstances give thanks, for this is the will of God for you in Christ Jesus." The Apostle makes it sound simple, but why do we struggle? We all deal with various forms of adversity. Some of us are unemployed, some are dealing with illness, and others are struggling with relationship or financial problems. The current economic crisis, the global attacks on religious liberties, and the relentless attacks on the Church by the secular media have made many of us gloomy and frightened. These are real obstacles to joy and they must be acknowledged, but as Romans 12:12 says: "Rejoice in hope, endure in affliction."

As tough as things may be, Catholics have work to do for Christ. Like the early Christians, we too are called to share the Good News. Do you recall that in the life of Saint Paul he was shipwrecked, imprisoned, beaten, starved, and stoned? He showed incredible fortitude to share his joy and the message of Christ to the gentiles despite his suffering. We should follow his example today.

For Catholics, joy in the midst of extreme adversity is our obligation and our duty. Remember that we are not alone. Our faith in Christ and our devotion in the sacraments that bind us to him will see us through the tough times and help us share a joy that will not evaporate in the face of tough challenges. Be encouraged by our Lord's words in John 16:33: "I have told you this so that you might have peace in me. In the world you will have trouble, but take courage, I have conquered the world."

It is so easy to get lost in our problems and forget to be joyful. It happens to me and just about everyone else I know. But remember that we are surrounded by people who are watching us. They may be seeking him and looking for someone—anyone—to show them the way to Christ. They could learn from our good example, be inspired by our joy, and be encouraged by our faith journeys if we will only remember that we are called to share the Good News. If we are gloomy, frustrated, inward-focused and critical of the Church, we will never be able to help anyone and may put our own salvation at risk.

Let me share four simple actions I try to follow in my desire to be joyful. This is by no means the definitive list, but this short checklist helps me stay on track:

- **Surrender to Christ every day** and recommit to putting him first in all areas of my life.

- **Give up my burdens to Jesus in daily prayer.** I can't do it alone and I need his help!

- **Be thankful for my blessings.** I can dwell on my problems or I can focus on all of the incredible blessings in my life and express my gratitude in prayer.

- **Start with the end in mind.** Are my actions each day serving him? I hope to hear Jesus say at the end of my life on earth, "Well done, good and faithful servant." My goal is heaven, and I must live a life that leads me there.

Do you find it difficult or easy to share your joy? I personally subscribe to the thinking of Archbishop Timothy Dolan of New York, who said: "Being Catholic is not a heavy burden, snuffing the joy out of life; rather our faith in Jesus and his Church gives meaning, purpose and joy to life."[31] Consider the simple manifestations of joy such as showing affection, smiling, laughter, joy after receiving the Eucharist in Mass or right after leaving reconciliation. The world will place enormous pressure on our shoulders that may make it feel impossible to be joyful at times, but if we are truly living our faith and trusting in Christ, then no burden or suffering will hold back the love that is in our hearts.

If I ever feel like I am not having a positive effect on the world, I can always show my sincere Christ-inspired joy to those I encounter each day in hopes of at least making a difference in the life of another person. That is a good place to start.

CHAPTER 21

Making a Difference

WANTED: Somebody to **Make a Difference**

*"Think about the possibilities if we all made a sincere
daily commitment, no matter how small, to make
a positive difference in the lives of those around us."*

DO WE SOMETIMES feel overwhelmed in the face of the relentless assault on the Church, our beliefs, and our families by the media and modern culture? Is it difficult to stand up for what we believe? Do we ever feel like we can't make a difference? Many Catholics I encounter are struggling through daily battles to live out their faith and protect their loved ones...all in the midst of a very difficult economic climate. It would be easy to throw in the towel and give up or remain silent, but that is not an option for us. We are called to do more. We are called to be holy: "Therefore in the Church, everyone whether belonging to the hierarchy, or being cared for by it, is called to holiness, according to the saying of the Apostle: 'For this is the will of God, your sanctification.'"[32]

Part of our challenge is getting past feeling overwhelmed. We are not able to tackle everything at once, so let's make it simple and focus on what we *can* do. We need to work on ourselves and pursue lives of personal holiness. Our ultimate destination is heaven, and we need to live our lives on earth in a way that will help us get there. So what can we do?

First of all, we can't stand on the sidelines and watch. We also must believe that one person can make a difference. Consider the examples of Blessed John Paul II, Saint Thérèse of Lisieux, Blessed Teresa of Calcutta, Saint Josemaria Escriva, and Saint Paul, to name a few. Our brave acts, no matter how small or large, can have a profound influence on others if we are simply willing to make the effort.

At times it seems we have lost our way and forgotten or ignored the teachings of the Church. Maybe we have forgotten to put our trust in God and rely on him. "Finally, draw your strength from the Lord and from his mighty power. Put on the armor of God so that you may be able to stand firm against the tactics of the devil. For our struggle is not with flesh and blood but with the principalities, with the powers, with the world rulers of this present darkness, with the evil spirits in the heavens. Therefore, put on the armor of God, that you may be able to resist on the evil day and, having done everything, to hold your ground" (Ephesians 6:10–13). I love the thought of putting on the "armor of God" as we fight the battles ahead!

Five Simple Ways Catholics Can Make a Difference

I am involved with a group of Catholic business leaders that meets every month. When we first started gathering in 2007, we had dreams of taking on the world and making a real difference through our Catholic faith! But we soon realized that we had much work to do in getting our spiritual lives in order. We understood after much prayer and reflection that we had to be humble and work on surrendering and conforming to Christ before we could make a positive difference in the lives of others. Here are five simple ways we have learned to make a difference in our lives and the lives of those around us:

- **Knowing what is necessary for spiritual growth.** We will not grow in our faith without daily prayer. We have to make prayer time a priority and stop making excuses. "The first rule for prayer, the most important first step, is not about how to do it, but to just do it; not to perfect and complete it but to begin it. Once the car is moving, it's easy to steer it in the right direction, but it's much harder to start it up when it's stalled. And prayer is stalled in our world."[33]

- **Remember we are called to lead lives of holiness.** As unpopular and out of step with our modern culture as this may be, we are all called to become saints. "The call to holiness is rooted in baptism and proposed anew in the other sacraments, principally in the Eucharist. Since Christians are reclothed in Christ Jesus and refreshed by his spirit, they are 'holy.' They therefore have the ability to manifest this holiness and the responsibility to bear witness to it in all that they do. The Apostle Paul never tires of admonishing all Christians to live 'as is fitting among saints' (Ephesians 5:3)."[34]

- **Live as a Catholic; speak as a Catholic.** We can't be cafeteria or cultural Catholics. We are called to live authentic Catholic lives and be true to our beautiful faith. "To acknowledge God before men is to be a living witness to his life and to his words. We want to fulfill our daily tasks, to carry out everything we do, according to the doctrine of Jesus Christ, and we should be disposed to make our faith transparent in every one of our family and professional obligations. Let us stop and think for a moment of our work, of our colleagues, of our friendships: are we seen as people whose lives are totally consistent with our faith?"[35]

- **We can't serve God AND the world.** We can't have it both ways. There is no way to pursue a life of holiness and worry about chasing illusory pleasures and the things of this world that don't matter. We can't serve God and the world at the same time.

- **Be a light for Christ to others.** One of the most profound ways to affect others is to radiate joy and let people see Christ at work in us. Our personal example can be the catalyst that helps lead someone into the Church. "Do everything without grumbling or questioning, that you may be blameless and innocent, children of God without blemish in the midst of a crooked and perverse generation, among whom you shine like lights in the world, as you hold on to the word of life, so that my boast for the day of Christ may be that I did not run in vain or labor in vain" (Philippians 2:14–16).

Where Catholics Are Called to Serve

The world needs Catholics to make a difference. How? Where have we been called to serve? Some of us are prayer warriors, silently praying in earnest for Mother Church, the sick, an end to abortion, and for the souls in purgatory (among other things). Some of us are called to the married or single life and still others are called to serve Christ in the public square. Many are called to the priesthood and religious life. Some are missionaries serving the poor and unwanted of the world. Wherever we are called, we have countless opportunities each day to serve him in our words and deeds. We should live out our calling with joy and know that our positive example will have an impact on the behavior and faith of others who are silently watching us.

As much as I try to give up my anxiety and fear in prayer, I am worried about the future of our country, the world, and the Church. I am inclined toward action and getting involved to make a difference, but I struggle sometimes to know how to apply my efforts. I have come to realize that I can best serve our Lord and his Church by being devoted in the practice of my Catholic faith and setting a good example. I need to be diligent about my prayer life as well as speaking up for what I believe. I have to be humble, loving, and remind myself that all of my efforts are for his greater glory and not my own.

Consider the wisdom in this quote from one of my favorite writers, Francis Fernandez, and his wonderful series of books *In Conversation with God*: "However, God does not ask the majority of Christians to shed their blood in testimony of the faith they profess. But he does ask of everyone an heroic steadfastness in proclaiming the truth through his life and words in environments which may be difficult and hostile to the teachings of Christ. He asks them to live fully the Christian virtues in the middle of the world, in whatever circumstances life has placed them. This is the path that the majority of Christians will have to tread—Christians who have to sanctify themselves through living heroism in the duties and circumstances of each day. Today's Christian needs the virtue of fortitude in a special way. This virtue, as well as being humanly so attractive, is indispensable given the materialistic mentality of so many people today; it is a mentality that prizes comfort and has a horror of anything that smacks of mortification, renunciation or sacrifice. So every act of virtue contains within it an act of courage, of fortitude; without it we cannot remain faithful to God."[36]

I find myself just as challenged as most people to live an authentic Catholic life in the world today. But I know we are called to try and make a sincere effort. I also know we are not alone and Christ stands ready to help us if we go to him in prayer with our desires. The key is to leave the sidelines and get started. Our efforts may be listening to a lonely and depressed coworker, saying a prayer for a friend seeking employment, or spending quality time with our family. Maybe now is the time to volunteer for a parish ministry. Whatever we do, let's do it to glorify Christ, put our fears aside, and truly serve him. Think about the possibilities if we all made a sincere daily commitment, no matter how small, to make a positive difference in the lives of those around us. The world would be transformed.

CHAPTER 22

The Integrated Catholic Life

The Power of Yes and the **Integrated Catholic Life**

"I flipped a switch, surrendered control,
and began to follow his lead. It was exhausting
to go it alone for over two decades,
and I needed his help."

NOT LONG AGO, an old college friend I had not seen in years asked me an interesting question: "How did you make such a profound change in your life?"

This person, who knew me more than twenty years ago from our wild days at the University of Georgia, wondered how I could have gone from a carefree, hedonistic lifestyle with an aversion to any kind of faith, to the father, husband, business person, and devout Catholic I am working hard to become. Knowing how I lived my life back in those days, I could understand the confusion.

Before I share with you how I answered this question, I want to remind you of my conversion story in the first two chapters. I grew up as a Southern Baptist but stopped attending that church at the age of sixteen. I then spent the next twenty-three years hiding from God and willfully trying to be in control of my life without his help. I led a compartmentalized existence and tried to balance work and family without the influence of any kind of faith.

Now, I will tell you how I answered my old college friend's question on the profound change in my life: "I stopped saying no to Christ and started saying *yes.*"

It really was that simple. I flipped a switch, surrendered control and began to follow his lead. It was exhausting to go it alone for more than two decades, and I knew in that life-changing Mass in 2005 that I needed his help. I realize now that saying "yes" is very liberating. It has allowed me to follow the teachings of the Church without question. I don't get bogged down in unproductive debates or practice cafeteria Catholicism. My full understanding of our Catholic faith may take a lifetime, but I have chosen to trust in the Church's teachings and the Holy Father's role as our guiding shepherd. I find myself looking for ways to serve Christ instead of argue with him.

The power of a simple "yes" has been the catalyst for me to become a better father, husband, and leader. As I shared in chapter three, now Christ comes first, followed by family, and work is third…and all the pieces click because I stopped trying to be in charge. I have learned to be humble and remember vividly that the first time I surrendered everything to Christ in 2005 I experienced a surge of strength and peace that has driven me forward in my faith journey ever since.

When I experienced my conversion, the seeds of my passion for the "integrated life" were sown. I had committed to put Christ first in all areas of my life and I realized that the compartmental-ized existence I once lived would no longer suffice. One of the key realizations I have had on my journey is the need to always keep my priorities straight and recommit to them frequently as I shared in chapter three. I have also realized that I will never achieve the inte-grated Catholic life I am pursuing unless I say "yes" and surrender to Christ on an ongoing basis.

From those very early days I began working with or starting Catholic ministries that supported this concept of integration. I also began writing and speaking on this topic in an effort to help other Catholics fully live out their faith in all areas of their lives. From the business world where I spend my time meeting new people every day to the ministry events I help lead and the school events and sports practices for my children where I encounter an endless stream of neighbors and friends, I am blessed to encounter many people who desire this integrated life for themselves. They often have a desire to strengthen their faith and be more authentically Catholic at work and in the public square, but are not sure how to begin.

One of the first things I read as I considered joining the Church in 2005 was this paragraph by Blessed John Paul II, who wrote in his apostolic exhortation *Christifideles Laici*: "The fundamental objective of the formation of the lay faithful is an ever-clearer discovery of one's vocation and the ever-greater willingness to live it so as to fulfill one's mission....The lay faithful, in fact, 'are called by God so that they, led by the spirit of the Gospel, might contribute to the sanctification of the world, as from within like leaven, by fulfilling their own particular duties. Thus, especially in this way of life, resplendent in faith, hope, and charity they manifest Christ to others.'"[37] The mission of the lay faithful forces us to consider the workplace the public square and everywhere else as fertile ground in which to do God's work. As we know from numerous Scripture passages and Church teaching, we are all called to lead lives of holiness and to be witnesses for Christ. Our vocations are necessarily a critical component of responding to that call.

There are numerous obstacles preventing the integration of our faith with our daily lives, especially work, but in my experience three of them consistently surface: silos, time and surrender. Let's "unpack" each of these obstacles:

Obstacle No. 1: Silos

Having operated within silos for my most of my life, I have learned how to recognize this challenge in others, and it is very, very common. Yet, I would suggest that many of us desire a more integrated life, a life in which Christ is at the center of our daily thoughts and actions at work and at home.

I believe that promoting this integration will help us all become better Christians and reverse the negative effects—emotional, moral, and spiritual—of keeping our faith separate from the rest of our lives. My friend Charlie Douglas—an author, speaker, and senior executive with a leading banking institution—says: "Perhaps part of the problem today is that there is a growing cultural demarcation between the sacred and the secular. Increasingly, love and faith are reserved for Church on Sundays, while the workplace demands a focused self-interest and a competitive edge to survive."

Overcoming this obstacle is not easy, but following the guidance I shared earlier from Blessed John Paul II's words in *Christifideles Laici,* we must see our daily activities, including our work, as opportunities to join ourselves to God and serve his will. We all play multiple roles in life: parents, spouses, siblings, leaders, employees, students, etc. But, the most important role and responsibility we have is to be faithful Catholics. Being faithful Catholics in *thought, word,* and *deed* at all times will allow us to seamlessly unify our lives and transcend our natural tendencies toward compartmentalization. Easy to say, possibly difficult to do...but necessary nonetheless.

Obstacle No. 2: Time

Do you struggle, as I shared in chapter thirteen, with having enough time each day? Most days my calendar is completely filled with meetings and phone calls. Outside of the workday, I am focused on helping my wife get the kids ready for school, family dinner time, evening time with the kids, youth sports, bedtime reading and prayers with the kids, time with my wife, infrequent exercise, answering e-mails I couldn't get to during the day, and then falling asleep exhausted after reading three pages of the book that has been on my nightstand for three months! Sound familiar?

Now, let's discuss what is more important than everything else I just mentioned: Christ and our relationship with him. The key here is to recognize that Christ should never compete for our time and that living our busy lives and putting him first are NOT mutually exclusive! He is not to be considered an *addition* to our lives....He is the *reason* for our lives. If we recall the point I made about the need to remove our silos, then we need to integrate our lives with Christ at the center of everything we do instead of viewing the daily practice of our faith as adding more time to already packed schedules.

Obstacle No. 3: Surrender

Surrender—giving up control of our lives to Christ—is an enormous obstacle to living out our faith in the workplace or any place for that matter. I remember very well what my life was like before surrendering to the Lord and putting him first in my life in 2005. All I had was family and work prior to that point, and I was in charge (I thought) of my own destiny. I dealt with life's challenges as they came and pridefully took the credit when things were going well. I thought I was being the strong husband and father that my father had been when I was growing up. I thought I was in control. But God had other ideas for me, and I came to realize how foolish I was to think my petty plans and goals could supersede the plans of our heavenly Father.

Please know that I still struggle with pride and placing Christ first in every aspect of my life. I have challenges like everyone else. But knowing that he will forgive me, love me, guide me, and bless me keeps me coming back again and again to the place where I pray the words, "I surrender Lord, please lead me." Surrendering to Christ is the key to overcoming the other obstacles of silos and time.

You may face different challenges to leading an integrated life, but these obstacles have consistently been issues for me and countless others I have encountered on my faith journey.

The integrated Catholic life requires the humility and self-awareness that comes from prayer and the guidance of the Holy Spirit in order to become real. The integrated Catholic life requires patience and discernment for as much as we may desire to go out and change the world, we need to be mindful of the need to change ourselves first. The integrated Catholic life requires ongoing surrender to Christ and the commitment to make him the center of our lives, *not* an addition to our lives.

As we travel toward our heavenly home, let us consider the incredible effect we could create in our lives and the lives of those we encounter if we all put our pride aside, surrendered and said "yes!" to Jesus, starting right now.

CONCLUSION

Where Will This Journey Lead Me?

I REMEMBER WELL the advice I was given by a wise priest in the early days of my joining the Church: "Randy, you need to remember that knowledge and understanding often follow repetition and action." His point was that I needed to go forward in my prayer life, my spiritual reading, and my study of Scripture and that knowledge and understanding would reveal itself over time. Over the years, this advice has helped me grow in my faith despite continued sinful behavior and other obstacles, often of my own making. For example, my repeated praying of the rosary has drawn me closer to the Blessed Mother, and I have come to rely on her intercession. Since my conversion, I have devoured books by Dr. Peter Kreeft, Father Thomas Dubay, Scott Hahn, Francis Fernandez, Blessed John Paul II, Pope Benedict XVI, and many others in an ongoing effort to grow in my Catholic faith. I read the Bible and catechism, although admittedly less frequently than I should. I have been going to eucharistic adoration at 5 a.m. every Wednesday since 2007, and this hour of prayer and reflection before the blessed sacrament has become the best hour of my week and the catalyst for much of the growth of my prayer life.

My love of Christ and his Church, a passion for learning, and a desire to grow have kept me going in the right direction. I often feel impatient with my progress and I pray frequently for patience and peace. Although journeys often have an end, mine simply has a destination—a destination that will take me a lifetime to reach:

heaven. I often reflect on my life before my conversion and shake my head at my stubborn and willful resistance to the role Christ needed to play in my life. I used to think that I had wasted those twenty-three years I spent away from God, but now I believe I was not ready back then for what our Lord had in store for me. When I was ready to put my pride aside and surrender, I had exhausted my own efforts and was fully prepared to acknowledge that he was in charge. My experiences before conversion have certainly shaped me. Perhaps I have a greater appreciation for the Truth I have found as a Catholic because of those challenging years.

Everyone is on a path to somewhere. If you have read this book, you may feel that something has been missing from your life and you are on a journey to find it. I can share with great certainty that the world does not hold the answers. There are numerous traps and obstacles on the path the world wants us to follow, and we are being continually lured away from our heavenly home by materialistic, morally depraved, and relativistic messages. True courage is turning our backs on the world, following Christ, and living integrated, authentic Catholic lives. This path will be the lonelier road, and there will be a steep price to pay. But isn't heaven worth it?

As I have shared throughout *Along the Way*, I don't pretend to have all the answers. I am a sinner who faces challenges, just like anyone else. One of the key goals for this book is to give readers a glimpse of an ordinary life, much like theirs, which has been made immeasurably better by surrendering to Christ and committing to following the teachings of the Catholic Church. I will still stumble and fall along the path before me, but I know where I want to be and will work diligently to get there with my family and everyone else I encounter.

Let's encourage and pray for each other as we travel down the road before us.

Endnotes

1   Saint Ignatius of Loyola, *Catholic Book of Quotations*, Leo Knowles, p. 163

2   *Catechism of the Catholic Church*, 2556

3   *Gaudium et Spes*, Second Vatican Council, 43

4   Chris Lowney, quoted on http://www.wharton.universia.net/index.cfm?fa=viewfeature&id=972&language=english

5   C.S. Lewis, *Mere Christianity*, p. 121

6   Francis Fernandez, *In Conversation with God*, Vol. 4, pp. 438 and 439, Section 72.1

7   *Lumen Gentium*, Second Vatican Council, 8 (74, 75, 76)

8   Father John A. Hardon, SJ, *The Real Presence* http://www.therealpresence.org/archives/Sin/Sin_010.htm

9   Attributed to Saint Alphonsus Liguori

10 *Catechism of the Catholic Church*, 1465

11 *Catechism of the Catholic Church*, 1422, LG 11 § 2.

12 Dr. Peter Kreeft, *Catholic Christianity: A Complete Catechism of Catholic Church Beliefs Based on the Catechism of the Catholic Church*, p. 112

13 Pope Benedict XVI, *Letter of the Holy Father to the Spanish Bishops*, July 8, 2006

14 Pope Benedict XVI, Address from Castel Gandolfo, October 1, 2006

15 John Paul II, *Redemptoris Missio*, Introduction, 3

16 *Lumen Gentium*, Second Vatican Council, 33

17 Francis Fernandez, *In Conversation with God,* Vol. 2, page 527, Section 85.1

18 Francis Fernandez, *In Conversation with God,* Vol. 2, page 333, Section 53.2

19 John Paul II, *Springtime of Evangelization,* p. 55

20 Pope Benedict XVI, *Message of His Holiness for Lent 2008,* October 30, 2007

21 John Paul II, Holy Mass at the Cathedral of St. Matthew, Homily of His Holiness John Paul II, Washington, October 6, 1979

22 Saint Augustine, *Catholic Book of Quotations,* Leo Knowles, p. 151

23 Francis Fernandez, *In Conversation with God,* Vol. 3, p. 259

24 *Catechism of the Catholic Church,* 2556

25 Code of Canon Law, Can. 898

26 Francis Fernandez, *In Conversation with God,* Vol. 4, pp. 267–268, Section 44.1

27 *Gaudium et Spes,* Second Vatican Council, 43

28 Attributed to Saint Francis of Assisi

29 Francis Fernandez, *In Conversation with God,* Vol. 4, p. 269, section 44.2

30 John Paul II, *Christifideles Laici,* Apostolic Exhortation, 17 (46), December 30, 1988

31 Archbishop Timothy Dolan, Op-Ed, *New York Daily News,* April 16, 2009

32 *Lumen Gentium,* Second Vatican Council, 39

33 Dr. Peter Kreeft, from the essay "Time," www.peterkreeft.com

34 John Paul II, *Christifideles Laici,* Apostolic Exhortation, 16

35 Francis Fernandez, *In Conversation with God,* Vol. 1, p. 44, Section 6.2

36 Francis Fernandez, *In Conversation with God,* Vol. 3, p. 208 Section 32.1

37 John Paul II, *Christifideles Laici,* Apostolic Exhortation, 58, 15 (37)